A YANKEE in MEXICAN CALIFORNIA 1834–1836

Richard Henry Dana Jr.

Foreword by John Seibert Farnsworth

Santa Clara University, Santa Clara, California
Heyday Books, Berkeley, California

Harper and Brothers originally published *Two Years Before the Mast* in 1840; in
1869, a revised version with a new appendix ("Twenty-Four Years After") by
the author was published by Fields, Osgood, and Co. in Boston. A new edition
published by Houghton and Mifflin Co. in 1911 included an introduction
("Seventy-Six Years After") by Dana's son, along with illustrations by E. Boyd
Smith. *A Yankee in Mexican California, 1834–1836*, uses the 1911 version of
the text and includes several of Ms. Smith's illustrations.

Now in the public domain, *Two Years Before the Mast* is widely available in
print and on the internet. The Modern Library edition (2001), introduced by
Gary Kinder, and the Penguin Classics edition (1981), edited and introduced
by Thomas Philbrick, both reproduce the original, 1840 version of the text.

Library of Congress Cataloging-in-Publication Data
Dana, Richard Henry, 1815-1882.
   [Two years before the mast. Selections]
   A Yankee in Mexican California, 1834-1836 / Richard Henry Dana ;
foreword by John Seibert Farnsworth.
       p. cm. -- (California legacy book)
   Originally published: Boston : Houghton Mifflin & Co., 1911.
   ISBN 978-1-59714-119-2 (pbk. : alk. paper)
   1. California--Description and travel. 2. California--History--To 1846. 3.
Voyages to the Pacific coast. 4. Dana, Richard Henry, 1815-1882--Travel--
California. I. Title.
   F864.D23 2010
   979.4'03--dc22
                                                2009019530

Cover Design: Lorraine Rath
Interior Design/Typesetting: Rebecca LeGates
Printing and Binding: Thomson-Shore, Dexter MI

This California Legacy book was copublished by Santa Clara University and
Heyday Books. Orders, inquiries, and correspondence should be addressed to:
              Heyday Books
              P. O. Box 9145, Berkeley, CA 94709
              (510) 549-3564, Fax (510) 549-1889
              www.heydaybooks.com

10 9 8 7 6 5 4 3 2 1

Contents

Foreword

John Seibert Farnsworth

It would be possible to read *Two Years Before the Mast* as a treatise on seeing rather than on sailing. The author—an undergraduate, of all things—temporarily abandons his studies at Harvard because of an eye condition brought on by a bout of measles. He can no longer see well enough to read his way through academia, and so he decides to see the world as a seaman. Despite a general lack of qualifications, he enlists as crew on a merchantman cargo vessel engaged in the hide trade. The year is 1834: Richard Henry Dana leaves Boston aboard the brig *Pilgrim* less than a fortnight after Charles Robert Darwin had arrived in Valparaiso aboard the ship *Beagle*.

As the title of his book indicates, Dana provides an eyewitness perspective from "before the mast," in other words, from the forecastle, which is where common sailors were berthed, the officers' quarters being located in relatively comfortable cabins further aft. Dana's perspective therefore stands unique among American letters; few denizens of the forecastle would have been literate in the days of sail, and even fewer would have been disposed to record their observations for publication. Then, even more than today, one would not expect to find a Harvard student in the forecastle of a brig.

Upon its publication in 1840, at the point when Dana had finally completed his studies and was admitted to the bar, the book became an instant success, drawing the attention of American intellectuals such as Ralph Waldo Emerson and Edgar Allan Poe, both of whom wrote reviews. Indeed, Emerson's review appeared in the inaugural issue of *The Dial*, where he predicted, "It will open the eyes of many to the conditions of the sailor, to the fearful waste of man....It will serve to hasten the day of reckoning between society and the sailor, which, though late, will not fail to come."

These were the heady days of the abolition movement, and *Two Years Before the Mast* resonated with the antislavery community because of Dana's account of the flogging of two of his fellow sailors by order of the *Pilgrim*'s authoritarian captain. The book sold ten thousand copies—blockbuster numbers in that era—and became a model for a number of politicized accounts, most notably Herman Melville's *White-Jacket*, set in oppressed forecastles.

History was doubly kind to the success of *Two Years Before the Mast*; nine years after the initial publication, gold was discovered in the hills of California, and the legendary rush was on. Thousands took to ships, brigs, clippers, and barques to round the Horn and ply their fortunes, and Dana's book comprised the only account in English that could acquaint these venturers with both their upcoming journey and its immediate destination. Melville himself advised, "But if you want the best idea of Cape Horn, get my friend Dana's unmatchable *Two Years Before the Mast*. But you can read, and so you must have read it. His chapters describing Cape Horn must have been written with an icicle."

Like Melville, most reviewers and critics over the years have focused on the more nautical aspects of Dana's masterpiece, especially on the maritime culture below decks. The result has been to obscure Dana's inimitable perceptions of the coastal landscape during the decade prior to the acquisition of California by the United States. The excerpt you hold in your hands remedies that oversight by omitting most of the forecastle material, thus focusing on Dana's California, a place to which sailors such as myself can never again navigate.

In Dana's California, the heavily forested San Francisco Bay Area is a fabulous place to collect firewood for the galley stoves, and Monterey is more picturesque than Santa Barbara because the adobes of the former village have been whitewashed while those of the latter "are mostly left of a mud color." San Pedro (the Port of Los Angeles) is "universally" considered the hell of Dana's California, while San Diego is nearest heaven because from there sailors embark on the return trip home, the holds of their vessels laden with hides for eastern markets.

Dana's perceptions are valuable not only because of their eyewitness nature but because they are informed by the attitudes and prejudices of an era humanity has all but transcended. The modern Californian will no doubt find Dana's characterizations of Californios, Indians,

Russians, and Hawaiians to be sexist, racist, classist, and colonialist. While reading through the selections of this edition, readers should remind themselves that the text herein was praised by some of the most progressive liberals of the era, including none other than Horace Mann, the educational reformer who was one of the most egalitarian, humanitarian voices of his age. We moderns can only conclude that our cultural landscape has changed as drastically as has the physical landscape that Dana describes.

There are certainly resonances between the California to which Dana sailed and the one whose waters I currently haunt. The "California fever" of which he complains has transmogrified into the laid-back "style" of which we Californians are so proud. My chauvinist pride swells further when I read Dana's observation that "revolutions are matters of frequent occurrence in California." Such is still the case, although the current spate of revolutions tend more toward the techno-cultural than the political. But some things never change: at one point Dana marvels, "We had now, out of forty or fifty, representatives of nearly every nation under the sun…" and he goes on to list a score of nationalities and ethnicities—a diverse spectrum every bit as colorful as the California we see today.

When Dana returned to San Francisco in 1859, nine years after California was admitted as the thirty-first state, he was welcomed as a celebrity. Perhaps, even then, the citizenry recognized him as the man whose perceptions, more than those of anyone else, had set the expectations for the California experience. As we once again view the nascent California through Dana's recovering eyes, let us celebrate how far we've come, all the while grieving whatever we've lost.

John Seibert Farnsworth
in San Francisco Bay aboard the sloop *Bashful*
Winter Solstice, 2008

An avid sailor, John Seibert Farnsworth is a professor of environmental writing and literature at Santa Clara University.

A
YANKEE
in MEXICAN
CALIFORNIA
1834–1836

Santa Barbara, January 1835

Upper California has the seat of its government at Monterey, where is also the custom-house, the only one on the coast, and at which every vessel intending to trade on the coast must enter its cargo before it can begin its traffic. We were to trade upon this coast exclusively, and therefore expected to go first to Monterey, but the captain's orders from home were to Santa Barbara, which is the central port of the coast, and wait there for the agent, who transacts all the business for the firm to which our vessel belonged.

The bay, or, as it was commonly called, the *canal* of Santa Barbara, is very large, being formed by the main land on one side (between Point Conception on the north and Point Santa Buenaventura on the south), which here bends in like a crescent, and by three large islands opposite to it and at the distance of some twenty miles. These points are just sufficient to give it the name of a bay, while

at the same time it is so large and so much exposed
to the southeast and northwest winds, that it is little
better than an open roadstead; and the whole swell of
the Pacific Ocean rolls in here before a southeaster, and
breaks with so heavy a surf in the shallow waters, that
it is highly dangerous to lie near in to the shore during
the southeaster season, that is, between the months of
November and April.

This wind (the southeaster) is the bane of the coast
of California. Between the months of November and
April (including a part of each), which is the rainy
season in this latitude, you are never safe from it; and
accordingly, in the ports which are open to it, vessels
are obliged, during these months, to lie at anchor at
a distance of three miles from the shore, with slip-
ropes on their cables, ready to slip and go to sea at a
moment's warning. The only ports which are safe from
this wind are San Francisco and Monterey in the north,
and San Diego in the south.

As it was January when we arrived, and the middle
of the southeaster season, we came to anchor at the distance of three miles from the shore, in eleven fathoms
water, and bent a slip-rope and buoys to our cables, cast
off the yard-arm gaskets from the sails, and stopped
them all with rope-yarns. After we had done this the
boat went ashore with the captain, and returned with
orders to the mate to send a boat ashore for him at
sundown. I did not go in the first boat, and was glad to
find that there was another going before night; for after
so long a voyage as ours had been, a few hours seem a
long time to be in sight and out of reach of land. We
spent the day on board in the usual duties; but as this

was the first time we had been without the captain, we felt a little more freedom, and looked about us to see what sort of a country we had got into, and were to pass a year or two of our lives in.

It was a beautiful day, and so warm that we wore straw hats, duck trousers, and all the summer gear. As this was midwinter, it spoke well for the climate; and we afterwards found that the thermometer never fell to the freezing point throughout the winter, and that there was very little difference between the seasons, except that during a long period of rainy and southeasterly weather, thick clothes were not uncomfortable.

The large bay lay about us, nearly smooth, as there was hardly a breath of wind stirring, though the boat's crew who went ashore told us that the long ground-swell broke into a heavy surf on the beach. There was only one vessel in the port—a long, sharp brig of about three hundred tons, with raking masts, and very square yards, and English colors at her peak. We afterwards learned that she was built at Guayaquil, and named the Ayacucho, after the place where the battle was fought that gave Peru her independence, and was now owned by a Scotchman named Wilson, who commanded her, and was engaged in the trade between Callao and other parts of South America and California. She was a fast sailer, as we frequently afterwards saw, and had a crew of Sandwich-Islanders on board. Beside this vessel, there was no object to break the surface of the bay. Two points ran out as the horns of the crescent, one of which—the one to the westward—was low and sandy, and is that to which vessels are obliged to give a wide berth when running out for a southeaster; the other is high, bold, and well wooded, and has a mission upon it, called Santa Buenaventura, from which the point is named. In the middle of this crescent, directly opposite the anchoring ground, lie the Mission and town of Santa Barbara, on a low plain, but little above the level of the sea, covered with grass, though entirely without trees, and surrounded on three sides by an amphitheatre of mountains, which slant off to the distance of fifteen or twenty miles. The Mission stands a little back of the town, and is a large building, or rather collection of buildings, in the centre of which is a high tower, with a belfry of five bells. The whole, being plastered, makes quite a show at a distance, and is the mark by which vessels come to anchor. The town lies a little nearer to the beach, —about half a mile from it, —and is composed of one-story houses built of sun-baked clay, or *adobe,* some of them whitewashed, with red tiles on the roofs. I should judge that there were about a hundred of them; and in the midst of them stands the Presidio, or fort, built of the same materials, and apparently but little stronger. The town is finely situated, with a bay in front, and an amphitheatre of hills behind. The only thing which diminishes its beauty is, that the hills have no large trees upon them, they having been all burnt by a great fire which swept them off about a dozen years ago, and they had not yet grown again. The fire was described to me by an inhabitant, as having been a very terrible and magnificent sight. The air of the whole valley was so heated that the people were obliged to leave the town and take up their quarters for several days upon the beach.

Just before sundown, the mate ordered a boat's crew ashore, and I went as one of the number. We passed under the stern of the English brig, and had a long pull ashore. I shall never forget the impression which our first landing on the beach of California made upon me. The sun had just gone down; it was getting dusky; the damp night-wind was beginning to blow, and the heavy swell of the Pacific was setting in, and breaking in loud and high "combers" upon the beach. We lay on our oars in the swell, just outside of the surf, waiting for a good chance to run in, when a boat, which had put off from the Ayacucho, came alongside of us, with a crew of dusky Sandwich-Islanders, talking and hallooing in their outlandish tongue. They knew that we were novices in this kind of boating, and waited to see us go in. The second mate, however, who steered our boat, determined to have the advantage of their experience, and would not go in first. Finding, at length, how matters stood, they gave a shout, and taking advantage of a great comber which came swelling in, rearing its head, and lifting up the sterns of our boats nearly perpendicular, and again dropping them in the trough, they gave three or four long and strong pulls, and went in on top of the great wave, throwing their oars overboard, and as far from the boat as they could throw them, and, jumping out the instant the boat touched the beach, they seized hold of her by the gunwale, on each side, and ran her up high and dry upon the sand. We saw, at once, how the thing was to be done, and also the necessity of keeping the boat stern out to the sea; for the instant the sea should strike upon her broadside or quarter, she would be driven up broadside on, and capsized. We pulled strongly in, and as soon as we felt that the sea had got hold of us, and was carrying us in with the speed of a race-horse, we threw the oars as far from the boat as we could, and took hold of the gunwales, ready to spring out and seize her when she struck, the officer using his utmost strength, with his steering-oar, to keep her stern out. We were shot up upon the beach, and, seizing the boat, ran her up high and dry, and, picking up our oars, stood by her, ready for the captain to come down.

Finding that the captain did not come immediately, we put our oars in the boat, and, leaving one to watch it, walked about the beach to see what we could of the place. The beach is nearly a mile in length between the two points, and of smooth sand. We had taken the only good landing-place, which is in the middle, it being more stony toward the ends. It is about twenty yards in width from high-water mark to a slight bank at which the soil begins, and so hard that it is a favorite place for running horses. It was growing dark, so that we could just distinguish the dim outlines of the two vessels in the offing; and the great seas were rolling in, in regular lines, growing larger and larger as they approached the shore, and hanging over the beach upon which they were to break, when their tops would curl over and turn white with foam, and, beginning at one extreme of the line, break rapidly to the other, as a child's long card house falls when a card is knocked down at one end. The Sandwich-Islanders, in the mean time, had turned their boat round, and ran her down into the water, and were loading her with hides and tallow. As this was the work in which we were soon to be engaged, we looked on with some curiosity. They ran the boat so far into the water that every large sea might float her, and two of them, with their trousers rolled up, stood by the bows, one on each side, keeping her in her right position. This was hard work; for beside the force they had to use upon the boat, the large seas nearly took them off their legs. The others were running from the boat to the bank, upon which, out of the reach of the water, was a pile of dry bullocks' hides, doubled lengthwise in the middle, and nearly as stiff as boards. These they took upon their heads, one or two at a time, and carried down to the boat, in which one of their number stowed them away. They were obliged to carry them on their heads, to keep them out of the water, and we observed that they had on thick woollen caps. "Look here, Bill, and see what you're coming to!" said one of our men to another who stood by the boat. "Well, Dana," said the second mate to me, "this does not look much like Harvard College, does it? But it is what I call *'head work.'*" To tell the truth, it did not look very encouraging.

Monterey

The bay of Monterey is wide at the entrance, being about twenty-four miles between the two points, Año Nuevo at the north, and Pinos at the south, but narrows gradually as you approach the town, which is situated in a bend, or large cove, at the south-eastern extremity, and from the points about eighteen miles, which is the whole depth of the bay. The shores are extremely well wooded (the pine abounding upon them), and as it was now the rainy season, everything was as green as nature could make it, —the grass, the leaves, and all; the birds were singing in the woods, and great numbers of wild fowl were flying over our heads. Here we could lie safe from the southeasters. We came to anchor within two cable lengths of the shore, and the town lay directly before us, making a very pretty appearance; its houses being of whitewashed adobe, which gives a much better effect than those of Santa Barbara, which are mostly left of a mud color. The red tiles, too, on the roofs, contrasted well with the white sides, and with the extreme greenness of the lawn upon which the houses—about a hundred in number—were dotted about, here and there, irregularly. There are in this place, and in every other town which I saw in California, no streets nor fences (except that here and there a small patch might be fenced in for a garden), so that the houses are placed at random upon the green. This, as they are of one story, and of the cottage form, gives them a pretty effect when seen from a little distance.

It was a fine Saturday afternoon that we came to anchor, the sun about an hour high, and everything looking pleasantly. The Mexican flag was flying from the little square Presidio, and the drums and trumpets of the soldiers, who were out on parade, sounded over the water, and gave great life to the scene. Every one was delighted with the appearance of things. We felt as though we had got into a Christian (which in the sailor's vocabulary means civilized) country. The first impression which California had made upon us was very disagreeable, —the open roadstead of Santa Barbara; anchoring three miles from the shore; running out to sea before every south-easter; landing in a high surf; with a little dark-looking town, a mile from the beach; and not a sound to be heard, nor anything to be seen, but Kanakas [Sandwich-Islanders], hides, and tallow-bags. Add to this the gale off Point Conception, and no one can be at a loss to account for our agreeable disappointment in Monterey. Besides, we soon learned, which was of no small importance to us, that there was little or no surf here, and this afternoon the beach was as smooth as a pond.

[...]

The next day we were "turned-to" early, and began taking off the hatches, overhauling the cargo, and getting everything ready for inspection. At eight, the officers of the customs, five in number, came on board, and began examining the cargo, manifest, &c. The Mexican revenue laws are very strict, and require the whole cargo to be landed, examined, and taken on board again; but our agent had succeeded in compounding for the last two vessels, and saving the trouble of taking the cargo ashore. The officers were dressed in the costume which we found prevailed through the country, —broad-brimmed hat, usually of a black or dark brown color, with a gilt or figured band round the crown, and lined under the rim with silk; a short jacket of silk, of figured calico (the European skirted body-coat is never worn); the shirt open in the neck; rich waistcoat, if any; pantaloons open at the sides below the knee, laced with gilt, usually of velveteen or broadcloth; or else short breeches and white stockings. They wear the deer-skin shoe, which is of a dark brown color, and (being made by Indians) usually a good deal ornamented. They have no suspenders, but always wear a sash round the waist, which is generally red, and varying in quality with the means of the wearer. Add to this the never-failing poncho, or the serapa, and you have the dress of the Californian. This last garment is always a mark of the rank and wealth of the owner. The *gente de razón,* or better sort of people, wear cloaks of black or dark blue broadcloth, with as much velvet and trimmings as may be; and from this they go down to the blanket of the Indian, the middle classes wearing a poncho, something like a large square cloth, with a hole in the middle for the head to go through. This is often as coarse as a blanket, but being beautifully woven with various colors, is quite showy at a distance. Among the Mexicans there is no working class (the Indians being practically serfs, and doing all the hard work); and every rich man looks like a grandee, and every poor scamp like a broken-down gentleman. I have often seen a man with a fine figure and courteous manners, dressed in broadcloth and velvet, with a noble horse completely covered with trappings, without a *reál* in his pockets, and absolutely suffering for something to eat.

[...]

The next day, the cargo having been entered in due form, we began trading. The trade-room was fitted up in the steerage, and furnished out with the lighter goods, and with specimens of the rest of the cargo; and Mellus, a young man who came out from Boston with us before the mast, was taken out of the forecastle, and made supercargo's clerk. He was well qualified for this business, having been clerk in a counting-house in Boston; but he had been troubled for some time with rheumatism, which unfitted him for the wet and exposed duty of a sailor on the coast. For a week or ten days all was life on board. The people came off to look and to buy, —men, women, and children; and we were continually going in the boats, carrying goods and passengers, —for they have no boats of their own. Everything must dress itself and come aboard and see the new vessel, if it were only to buy a paper of pins. The agent and his clerk managed the sales, while we were busy in the hold or in the boats. Our cargo was an assorted one; that is, it consisted of everything under the sun. We had spirits of all kinds (sold by the cask), teas, coffee, sugars, spices, raisins, molasses, hardware, crockery-ware, tin-ware, cutlery, clothing of all kinds, boots and shoes from Lynn, calicoes and cotton from Lowell, crapes, silks; also, shawls, scarfs, necklaces, jewelry, and combs for the women; furniture; and, in fact, everything that can be imagined, from Chinese fireworks to English cart-wheels, —of which we had a dozen pairs with their iron tires on.

The Californians are an idle, thriftless people, and can make nothing for themselves. The country abounds in grapes, yet they buy, at a great price, bad wine made in Boston and brought round by us, and retail it among themselves at a reál (12½ cents) by the small wineglass. Their hides, too, which they value at two dollars in money, they barter for something which costs seventy-five cents in Boston; and buy shoes (as like as not made of their own hides, which have been carried twice round Cape Horn) at three and four dollars, and "chicken-skin boots" at fifteen dollars a pair. Things sell, on an average, at an advance of nearly three hundred per cent upon the Boston prices. This is partly owing to the heavy duties which the government, in their wisdom, with an idea, no doubt, of keeping the silver in the country, has laid upon imports. These duties, and the enormous expenses of so long a voyage, keep all merchants but those of heavy capital from engaging in the trade. Nearly two thirds of all the articles imported into the country from round Cape Horn, for the last six years, have been by the single house of Bryant, Sturgis, & Co., to whom our vessel belonged and who have a permanent agent on the coast.

This kind of business was new to us, and we liked it very well for a few days, though we were hard at work every minute from daylight to dark, and sometimes even later.

By being thus continually engaged in transporting passengers, with their goods, to and fro, we gained considerable knowledge of the character, dress, and language of the people. The dress of the men was as I have before described it. The women wore gowns of various texture, —silks, crape, calicoes, &c., —made after the European style, except that the sleeves were short, leaving the arm bare, and that they were loose about the waist, corsets not being in use. They wore shoes of kid or satin, sashes or belts of bright colors, and almost always a necklace and ear-rings. Bonnets they had none. I only saw one on the coast, and that belonged to the wife of an American sea-captain who had settled in San Diego, and had imported the chaotic mass of straw and ribbon, as a choice present to his new wife. They wear their hair (which is almost invariably black, or a very dark brown) long in their necks, sometimes loose, and sometimes in long braids; though the married women often do it up on a high comb. Their only protection against the sun and weather is a large mantle which they put over their heads, drawing it close round their faces, when they go out of doors, which is generally only in pleasant weather. When in the house, or sitting out in front of it, which they often do in fine weather, they usually wear a small scarf or neckerchief of a rich pattern. A band, also, about the top of the head, with a cross, star, or other ornament in front, is common. Their complexions are various, depending—as well as their dress and manner—upon the amount of Spanish blood they can lay claim to, which also settles their social rank. Those who are of pure Spanish blood, having never intermarried with the aborigines, have clear brunette complexions, and sometimes even as fair as those of English women. There are but few of these families in California, being mostly those in official stations, or who, on the expiration of their terms of office, have settled here upon property they have acquired; and others who have been banished for state offences. These form the upper class, intermarrying, and keeping up an exclusive system in every respect. They can be distinguished, not only by their complexion, dress, and manners, but also by their speech; for, calling themselves Castilians, they are very ambitious of speaking the pure Castilian, while all Spanish is spoken in a somewhat corrupted dialect by the lower classes. From this upper class, they go down by regular shades, growing more and more dark and muddy, until you come to the pure Indian, who runs about with nothing upon him but a small piece of cloth, kept up by a wide leather strap drawn round his waist. Generally speaking, each person's caste is decided by the quality of the blood, which shows itself, too plainly to be concealed, at first sight. Yet the least drop of Spanish blood, if it be only of quadroon or octoroon, is sufficient to raise one from the position of a serf, and entitle him to wear a suit of clothes, —boots, hat, cloak, spurs, long knife, all complete, though coarse and dirty as may be, —and to call himself Español, and to hold property, if he can get any.

The fondness for dress among the women is excessive, and is sometimes their ruin. A present of a fine mantle, or of a necklace or pair of ear-rings, gains the favor of the greater part. Nothing is more common than to see a woman living in a house of only two rooms, with the ground for a floor, dressed in spangled satin shoes, silk gown, high comb, and gilt, if not gold, ear-rings and necklace. If their husbands do not dress them well enough, they will soon receive presents from others. They used to spend whole days on board our vessel, examining the fine clothes and ornaments, and frequently making purchases at a rate which would have made a seamstress or waiting-maid in Boston open her eyes.

Next to the love of dress, I was most struck with the fineness of the voices and beauty of the intonations of both sexes. Every common ruffian-looking fellow, with a slouched hat, blanket cloak, dirty under-dress, and soiled leather leggins, appeared to me to be speaking elegant Spanish. It was a pleasure simply to listen to the sound of the language, before I could attach any meaning to it. They have a good deal of the Creole drawl, but it is varied by an occasional extreme rapidity of utterance, in which they seem to skip from consonant to consonant, until, lighting upon a broad, open vowel, they rest upon that to restore the balance of sound. The women carry this peculiarity of speaking to a much greater extreme than the men, who have more evenness and stateliness of utterance. A common bullock-driver, on horseback, delivering a message, seemed to speak like an ambassador at a royal audience. In fact, they sometimes appeared to me to be a people on whom a curse had fallen, and stripped them of everything but their pride, their manners, and their voices.

Another thing that surprised me was the quantity of silver in circulation. I never, in my life, saw so much silver at one time, as during the week that we were at Monterey. The truth is, they have no credit system, no banks, and no way of investing money but in cattle. Besides silver, they have no circulating medium but hides, which the sailors call "California bank-notes." Everything that they buy they must pay for by one or the other of these means. The hides they bring down dried and doubled, in clumsy ox-carts, or upon mules' backs, and the money they carry tied up in a handkerchief, fifty or a hundred dollars and half-dollars.

I had not studied Spanish at college, and could not speak a word when at [the island group called] Juan Fernandez; but, during the latter part of the passage out, I borrowed a grammar and dictionary from the cabin, and by a continual use of these, and a careful attention to every word that I heard spoken, I soon got a vocabulary together, and began talking for myself. As I soon knew more Spanish than any of the crew (who, indeed, knew none at all), and had studied Latin and French, I got the name of a great linguist, and was always sent by the captain and officers for provisions, or to take letters and messages to different parts of the town. I was often sent for something which I could not tell the name of to save my life; but I liked the business, and accordingly never pleaded ignorance. Sometimes I managed to jump below and take a look at my dictionary before going ashore; or else I overhauled some English resident on my way, and learned the word from him; and then, by signs, and by giving a Latin or French word a twist at the end, contrived to get along. This was a good exercise for me, and no doubt taught me more than I should have learned by months of study and reading; it also gave me opportunities of seeing the customs, characters, and domestic arrangements of the people, beside being a great relief from the monotony of a day spent on board ship.

Monterey, as far as my observation goes, is decidedly the pleasantest and most civilized-looking place in California. In the centre of it is an open square, surrounded by four lines of one-story buildings, with half a dozen cannon in the centre; some mounted, and others not. This is the Presidio, or fort. Every town has a presidio in its centre; or rather every presidio has a town built around it; for the forts were first built by the Mexican government, and then the people built near them, for protection. The presidio here was entirely open and unfortified. There were several officers with long titles, and about eighty soldiers, but they were poorly paid, fed, clothed, and disciplined. The governor-general, or, as he is commonly called, the "general," lives here, which makes it the seat of government. He is appointed by the central government at Mexico, and is the chief civil and military officer. In addition to him, each town has a commandant who is its chief officer, and has charge of the fort, and of all transactions with foreigners and foreign vessels; while two or three alcaldes and corregidores, elected by the inhabitants, are the civil officers. Courts strictly of law, with a system of jurisprudence, they have not. Small municipal matters are regulated by the alcaldes and corregidores, and everything relating to the general government, to the military, and to foreigners, by the commandants, acting under the governor-general. Capital cases are decided by the latter, upon personal inspection, if near; or upon minutes sent him by the proper officers, if the offender is at a distant place. No Protestant has any political rights, nor can he hold property, or, indeed, remain more than a few weeks on shore, unless he belong to a foreign vessel. Consequently, Americans and English, who intend to reside here, become Papists, —the current phrase among them being, "A man must leave his conscience at Cape Horn."

But, to return to Monterey. The houses here, as everywhere else in California, are of one story, built of adobes, that is, clay made into large bricks, about a foot and a half square, and three or four inches thick, and hardened in the sun. These are joined together by a cement of the same material, and the whole are of a common dirt-color. The floors are generally of earth, the windows grated and without glass; and the doors, which are seldom shut, open directly into the common room, there being no entries. Some of the more wealthy inhabitants have glass to their windows and board floors; and in Monterey nearly all the houses are whitewashed on the outside. The better houses, too, have red tiles upon the roofs. The common ones have two or three rooms which open into each other, and are furnished with a bed or two, a few chairs and tables, a looking-glass, a crucifix, and small daubs of paintings enclosed in glass, representing some miracle or martyrdom. They have no chimneys or fireplaces in the houses, the climate being such as to make a fire unnecessary; and all their cooking is done in a small kitchen, separated from the house. The Indians, as I have said before, do all the hard work, two or three being attached to the better house; and the poorest persons are able to keep one, at least, for they have only to feed them, and give them a small piece of coarse cloth and a belt for the men, and a coarse gown, without shoes or stockings, for the women.

In Monterey there are a number of English and Americans (English or Ingles all are called who speak the English language) who have married Californians, become united to the Roman Church, and acquired considerable property. Having more industry, frugality, and enterprise than the natives, they soon get nearly all the trade into their hands. They usually keep shops, in which they retail the goods purchased in larger quantities from our vessels, and also send a good deal into the interior, taking hides in pay, which they again barter with our ships. In every town on the coast there are foreigners engaged in this kind of trade, while I recollect but two shops kept by natives. The people are naturally suspicious of foreigners, and they would not be allowed to remain, were it not that they conform to the Church, and by marrying natives, and bringing up their children as Roman Catholics and Mexicans, and not teaching them the English language, they quiet suspicion, and even become popular and leading men. The chief alcaldes in Monterey and Santa Barbara were Yankees by birth.

The men in Monterey appeared to me to be always on horseback. Horses are as abundant here as dogs and chickens were in Juan Fernandez. There are no stables to keep them in, but they are allowed to run wild and graze wherever they please, being branded, and having long leather ropes, called lassos, attached to their necks and dragging along behind them, by which they can be easily taken. The men usually catch one in the morning, throw a saddle and bridle upon him, and use him for the day, and let him go at night, catching another the next day. When they go on long journeys, they ride one horse down, and catch another, throw the saddle and bridle upon him, and, after riding him down, take a third, and so on to the end of the journey. There are probably no better riders in the world. They are put upon a horse when only four or five years old, their little legs not long enough to come half-way over his sides, and may almost be said to keep on him until they have grown to him. The stirrups are covered or boxed up in front, to prevent their catching when riding through the woods; and the saddles are large and heavy, strapped very tight upon the horse, and have large pommels, or loggerheads, in front, round which the lasso is coiled when not in use. They can hardly go from one house to another without mounting a horse, there being generally several standing tied to the door-posts of the little cottages. When they wish to show their activity, they make no use of their stirrups in mounting, but, striking the horse, spring into the saddle as he starts, and, sticking their long spurs into him, go off on the full run. Their spurs are cruel things, having four or five rowels, each an inch in length, dull and rusty. The flanks of the horses are often sore from them, and

I have seen men come in from chasing bullocks, with their horses' hind legs and quarters covered with blood. They frequently give exhibitions of their horsemanship in races, bull-baitings, &c.; but as we were not ashore during any holiday, we saw nothing of it. Monterey is also a great place for cock-fighting, gambling of all sorts, fandangos, and various kinds of amusement and knavery. Trappers and hunters, who occasionally arrive here from over the Rocky Mountains, with their valuable skins and furs, are often entertained with amusements and dissipation, until they have wasted their opportunities and their money, and then go back, stripped of everything.

Nothing but the character of the people prevents Monterey from becoming a large town. The soil is as rich as man could wish, climate as good as any in the world, water abundant, and situation extremely beautiful. The harbor, too, is a good one, being subject only to one bad wind, the north; and though the holding-ground is not the best, yet I heard of but one vessel's being driven ashore here.

San Diego

The next day being Sunday, after washing and clearing decks, and getting breakfast, the mate came forward with leave for one watch to go ashore, on liberty. We drew lots, and it fell to the larboard, which I was in. Instantly all was preparation. Buckets of fresh water (which we were allowed in port), and soap, were put in use; go-ashore jackets and trousers got out and brushed; pumps, neckerchiefs, and hats overhauled, one lending to another; so that among the whole each got a good fit-out. A boat was called to pull the "liberty-men" ashore, and we sat down in the stern sheets, "as big as pay-passengers," and, jumping ashore, set out on our walk for the town, which was nearly three miles off.

It is a pity that some other arrangement is not made in merchant vessels with regard to the liberty-day. When in port, the crews are kept at work all the week, and the only day they are allowed for rest or pleasure is Sunday;

and unless they go ashore on that day, they cannot go at all. I have heard of a religious captain who gave his crew liberty on Saturdays, after twelve o'clock. This would be a good plan, if shipmasters would bring themselves to give their crews so much time. For young sailors especially, many of whom have been brought up with a regard for the sacredness of the day, this strong temptation to break it is exceedingly injurious. As it is, it can hardly be expected that a crew, on a long and hard voyage, will refuse a few hours of freedom from toil and the restraints of a vessel, and an opportunity to tread the ground and see the sights of society and humanity, because it is a Sunday. They feel no objection to being drawn out of a pit on the Sabbath day.

I shall never forget the delightful sensation of being in the open air, with the birds singing around me, and escaped from the confinement, labor, and strict rule of a vessel, —of being once more in my life, though only for a day, my own master. A sailor's liberty is but for a day; yet while it lasts it is entire. He is under no one's eye, and can do whatever, and go wherever, he pleases. This day, for the first time, I may truly say, in my whole life, I felt the meaning of a term which I had often heard, —the sweets of liberty. Stimson was with me, and, turning our backs upon the vessels, we walked slowly along, talking of the pleasure of being our own masters, of the times past, when we were free and in the midst of friends, in America, and of the prospect of our return; and planning where we would go, and what we would do, when we reached home. It was wonderful how the prospect brightened, and how short and tolerable the voyage appeared, when viewed in this new light. Things looked differently from

what they did when we talked them over in the little
dark forecastle, the night after the flogging, at San Pedro.
It is not the least of the advantages of allowing sailors
occasionally a day of liberty, that it gives them a spring,
and makes them feel cheerful and independent, and leads
them insensibly to look on the bright side of everything
for some time after.

Stimson and I determined to keep as much together
as possible, though we knew that it would not do to *cut*
our shipmates; for, knowing our birth and education, they
were a little suspicious that we would try to put on the
gentleman when we got ashore, and would be ashamed
of their company; and this won't do with Jack. When the
voyage is at an end, you do as you please; but so long as
you belong to the same vessel, you must be a shipmate
to him on shore, or he will not be a shipmate to you on
board. Being forewarned of this before I went to sea, I
took no "long togs" with me; and being dressed like the
rest, in white duck trousers, blue jacket, and straw hat,
which would prevent my going into better company, and
showing no disposition to avoid them, I set all suspicion
at rest. Our crew fell in with some who belonged to the
other vessels, and, sailor-like, steered for the first grog-
shop. This was a small adobe building, of only one room,
in which were liquors, "drygoods," West India goods,
shoes, bread, fruits, and everything which is vendible in
California. It was kept by a Yankee, a one-eyed man, who
belonged formerly to Fall River, came out to the Pacific
in a whale-ship, left her at the Sandwich Islands, and
came to California and set up a pulpería [small shop].
Stimson and I followed in our shipmates' wake, knowing
that to refuse to drink with them would be the highest

affront, but determining to slip away at the first opportunity. It is the universal custom with sailors for each one, in his turn, to treat the whole, calling for a glass all round, and obliging every one who is present, even to the keeper of the shop, to take a glass with him. When we first came in, there was some dispute between our crew and the others, whether the new-comers or the old California rangers should treat first; but it being settled in favor of the latter, each of the crews of the other vessels treated all round in their turn, and as there were a good many present (including some "loafers" who had dropped in, knowing what was going on, to take advantage of Jack's hospitality), and the liquor was a reál (12½ cents) a glass, it made somewhat of a hole in their lockers. It was now our ship's turn, and Stimson and I, desirous to get away, stepped up to call for glasses; but we soon found that we must go in order, —the oldest first, for the old sailors did not choose to be preceded by a couple of youngsters; and *bon gré, mal gré,* we had to wait our turn, with the twofold apprehension of being too late for our horses, and of getting too much; for drink you must, every time; and if you drink with one, and not with another, it is always taken as an insult.

Having at length gone through our turns and acquitted ourselves of all obligations, we slipped out, and went about among the houses, endeavoring to find horses for the day, so that we might ride round and see the country. At first we had but little success, all that we could get out of the lazy fellows, in reply to our questions, being the eternal drawling *Quien sabe?* ("Who knows?") which is an answer to all questions. After several efforts, we at length fell in with a little Sandwich-Island boy, who belonged to Captain Wilson, of the Ayacucho, and was well acquainted in the place; and he, knowing where to go, soon procured us two horses, ready saddled and bridled, each with a lasso coiled over the pommel. These we were to have all day, with the privilege of riding them down to the beach at night, for a dollar, which we had to pay in advance. Horses are the cheapest thing in California; very fair ones not being worth more than ten dollars apiece, and the poorer being often sold for three and four. In taking a day's ride, you pay for the use of the saddle, and for the labor and trouble of catching the horses. If you bring the saddle back safe, they care but little what becomes of the horse. Mounted on our horses, which were spirited beasts (and which, by the way, in this country, are always steered in the cavalry fashion, by pressing the contrary rein against the neck, and not by pulling on the bit), we started off on a fine run over the country. The first place we went to was the old ruinous presidio, which stands on a rising ground near the village, which it overlooks. It is built in the form of an open square, like all the other presidios, and was in a most ruinous state, with the exception of one side, in which the commandant lived, with his family. There were only two guns, one of which was spiked, and the other had no carriage. Twelve half-clothed and half-starved-looking fellows composed the garrison; and they, it was said, had not a musket apiece. The small settlement lay directly below the fort, composed of about forty dark brown looking huts, or houses, and three or four larger ones, whitewashed, which belonged to the "gente de razón." This town is not more than half as large as Monterey, or Santa Barbara, and has little or no business. From the presidio, we rode off in the direction of the Mission, which we were told was three miles distant. The country was rather sandy, and there was nothing for miles which could be called a tree, but the grass grew green and rank, there were many bushes and thickets, and the soil is said to be good. After a pleasant ride of a couple of miles, we saw the white walls of the Mission, and, fording a small stream, we came directly before it. The Mission is built of adobe and plastered. There was something decidedly striking in its appearance: a number of irregular buildings, connected with one another, and, disposed in the form of a hollow square, with a church at one end, rising above the rest, with a tower containing five belfries, in each of which hung a large bell, and with very large rusty iron crosses at the tops. Just outside of the buildings, and under the walls, stood twenty or thirty small huts, built of straw and of the branches of trees, grouped together, in which a few Indians lived, under the protection and in the service of the Mission.

Entering a gateway, we drove into the open square, in which the stillness of death reigned. On one side was the church; on another, a range of high buildings with grated windows; a third was a range of smaller buildings, or offices, and the fourth seemed to be little more than a high connecting wall. Not a living creature could we see. We rode twice round the square, in the hope of waking up some one; and in one circuit saw a tall monk, with shaven head, sandals, and the dress of the Gray Friars, pass rapidly through a gallery, but he disappeared without noticing us. After two circuits, we stopped our horses, and at last a man showed himself in front of one of the small buildings. We rode up to him, and found him dressed in the common dress of the country, with a silver chain round his neck, supporting a large bunch of keys. From this, we took him to be the steward of the Mission, and, addressing him as "Mayor-domo," received a low bow and an invitation to walk into his room. Making our horses fast, we went in. It was a plain room, containing a table, three or four chairs, a small picture or two of some saint, or miracle, or martyrdom, and a few dishes and glasses. "Hay alguna cosa de comer?" said I, from my grammar. "Si, Señor!" said he. "Que gusta usted?" Mentioning fríjoles, which I knew they must have if they had nothing else, and beef and bread, with a hint for wine, if they had any, he went off to another building across the court, and returned in a few minutes with a couple of Indian boys bearing dishes and a decanter of wine. The dishes contained baked meats, fríjoles stewed with peppers and onions, boiled eggs, and California flour baked into a kind of macaroni. These, together with the wine, made the most sumptuous meal we had eaten since we left Boston; and, compared with the fare we had lived upon for seven months, it was a regal banquet. After despatching it, we took out some money and asked him how much we were to pay. He shook his head, and crossed himself, saying that it was charity, —that the Lord gave it to us. Knowing the amount of this to be that he did not sell, but was willing to receive a present, we gave him ten or twelve reáls, which he pocketed with admirable nonchalance, saying, "Dios se lo pague." Taking leave of him, we rode out to the Indians' huts. The little children were running about among the huts, stark naked, and the men were not much more; but the women had generally coarse gowns of a sort of tow cloth. The men are employed, most of the time, in tending the cattle of the Mission, and in working in the garden, which is a very large one, including several acres, and filled, it is said, with the best fruits of the climate. [...]

Here, among the huts, we saw the oldest man that I had ever met with; and, indeed, I never supposed that a person could retain life and exhibit such marks of age. He was sitting out in the sun, leaning against the side of a hut; and his legs and arms, which were bare, were of a dark red color, the skin withered and shrunk up like burnt leather, and the limbs not larger round than those of a boy of five years. He had a few gray hairs, which were tied together at the back of his head, and he was so feeble that, when we came up to him, he raised his hands slowly to his face, and, taking hold of his lids with his fingers, lifted them up to look at us; and, being satisfied, let them drop again. All command over the lids seemed to have gone. I asked his age, but could get no answer but "Quien sabe?" and they probably did not know it.

Leaving the Mission, we returned to the village, going nearly all the way on a full run. The California horses have no medium gait, which is pleasant, between walking and running; for as there are no streets and parades, they have no need of the genteel trot, and their riders usually keep them at the top of their speed until they are tired, and then let them rest themselves by walking. The fine air of the afternoon, the rapid gait of the animals, who seemed almost to fly over the ground, and the excitement and novelty of the motion to us, who had been long confined on shipboard, were exhilarating beyond expression, and we felt willing to ride all day long. Coming into the village, we found things looking very lively. The Indians, who always have a holiday on Sunday, were engaged at playing a kind of running game of ball, on a level piece of ground, near the houses. The old ones sat down in a ring, looking on, while the young ones—men, boys, and girls—were chasing the ball, and throwing it with all their might. Some of the girls ran like greyhounds. At every accident, or remarkable feat, the old people set up a deafening screaming and clapping of hands. Several blue jackets were reeling about among the houses, which showed that the pulperías had been well patronized. One or two of the sailors had got on horseback, but being rather indifferent horsemen, and the Mexicans having given them vicious beasts, they were soon thrown, much to the amusement of the people. A half-dozen Sandwich-Islanders, from the hide-houses and the two brigs, bold riders, were dashing about on the full gallop, hallooing and laughing like so many wild men.

It was now nearly sundown, and Stimson and I went into a house and sat quietly down to rest ourselves before going to the beach. Several people soon collected to see "los marineros ingleses," and one of them, a young woman, took a great fancy to my pocket-handkerchief, which was a large silk one that I had before going to sea, and a handsomer one than they had been in the habit of seeing. Of course, I gave it to her, which brought me into high favor; and we had a present of some pears and other fruits, which we took down to the beach with us. When we came to leave the house, we found that our horses, which we had tied at the door, were both gone. We had paid for them to ride down to the beach, but they were not to be found. We went to the man of whom we hired them, but he only shrugged his shoulders, and to our question, "Where are the horses?" only answered, "Quien sabe?" but as he was very easy, and made no inquiries for the saddles, we saw that he knew very well where they were. After a little trouble, determined not to walk to the beach, —a distance of three miles, —we procured two, at four reáls more apiece, with two Indian boys to run behind and bring them back. Determined to have "the go" out of the horses, for our trouble, we went down at full speed, and were on the beach in a few minutes. Wishing to make our liberty last as long as possible, we rode up and down among the hide-houses, amusing ourselves with seeing the men as they arrived (it was now dusk), some on horseback and others on foot. The Sandwich-Islanders rode down, and were in "high snuff." We inquired for our shipmates, and were told that two of them had started on horseback, and been thrown, or had fallen off, and were seen heading for the beach, but steering pretty wild, and, by the looks of things, would not be down much before midnight.

The Indian boys having arrived, we gave them our horses, and, having seen them safely off, hailed for a boat, and went aboard. Thus ended our first liberty-day on shore. We were well tired, but had had a good time, and were more willing to go back to our old duties. About midnight we were waked up by our two watchmates, who had come aboard in high dispute. It seems they had started to come down on the same horse, double-backed; and each was accusing the other of being the cause of his fall. They soon, however, turned-in and fell asleep, and probably forgot all about it, for the next morning the dispute was not renewed.

Santa Barbara, San Juan Capistrano, and San Pedro, April 1835

The next Sunday was Easter, and as there had been no liberty at San Pedro, it was our turn to go ashore and misspend another Sabbath. Soon after breakfast, a large boat, filled with men in blue jackets, scarlet caps, and various-colored under-clothes, bound ashore on liberty, left the Italian ship, and passed under our stern, the men singing beautiful Italian boat-songs all the way, in fine, full chorus. Among the songs I recognized the favorite, "O Pescator dell'onda." It brought back to my mind piano-fortes, drawing-rooms, young ladies singing, and a thousand other things which as little befitted me, in my situation, to be thinking upon. Supposing that the whole day would be too long a time to spend ashore, as there was no place to which we could take a ride, we remained quietly on board until after dinner. We were then pulled ashore in the stern of the boat, —for it is a point with liberty-men to be pulled off and back as passengers by their shipmates, —and, with orders to be on the beach at sundown, we took our way for the town. There, everything wore the appearance of a holiday. The people were dressed in their best; the men riding about among the houses, and the women sitting on carpets before the doors. Under the piazza of a pulpería two men were seated, decked out with knots of ribbons and bouquets, and playing the violin and the Spanish guitar. These are the only instruments, with the exception of the drums and trumpets at Monterey, that I ever heard in California; and I suspect they play upon no others, for at a great *fandango* at which I was afterwards present, and where they mustered all the music they could find, there were three violins and two guitars, and no other instruments. As it was now too near the middle of the day to see any dancing, and hearing that a bull was expected down from the country, to be baited in the presidio square, in the course of an hour or two, we took a stroll among the houses. Inquiring for an American who, we had been told, had married in the place, and kept a shop, we were directed to a long, low building, at the end of which was a door, with a sign over it, in Spanish. Entering the shop, we found no one in it, and the whole had an empty, deserted air. In a few minutes the man made his appearance, and apologized for having nothing to entertain us with, saying that he had had a fandango at his house the night before, and the people had eaten and drunk up everything.

"O yes!" said I, "Easter holidays!"

"No!" said he, with a singular expression on his face; "I had a little daughter die the other day, and that's the custom of the country."

At this I felt somewhat awkwardly, not knowing what to say, and whether to offer consolation or not, and was beginning to retire, when he opened a side-door and told us to walk in. Here I was no less astonished; for I found a large room, filled with young girls, from three or four years of age up to fifteen and sixteen, dressed all in white, with wreaths of flowers on their heads, and bouquets in their hands. Following our conductor among these girls, who were playing about in high spirits, we came to a table, at the end of the room, covered with a white cloth, on which lay a coffin, about three feet long, with the body of his child. The coffin was covered with white cloth, and lined with white satin, and was strewn with flowers. Through an open door, we saw, in another room, a few elderly people in common dresses; while the benches and tables thrown up in a corner, and the stained walls, gave evident signs of the last night's "high go." Feeling, like [actor] Garrick, between Tragedy and Comedy, an uncertainty of purpose, I asked the man when the funeral would take place, and being told that it would move toward the Mission in about an hour, took my leave.

To pass away the time, we hired horses and rode to the beach, and there saw three or four Italian sailors, mounted, and riding up and down on the hard sand at a furious rate. We joined them, and found it fine sport. The beach gave us a stretch of a mile or more, and the horses flew over the smooth, hard sand, apparently invigorated and excited by the salt sea-breeze, and by the continual roar and dashing of the breakers. From the beach we

returned to the town, and, finding that the funeral
procession had moved, rode on and overtook it, about
half-way to the Mission. Here was as peculiar a sight as
we had seen before in the house, the one looking as much
like a funeral procession as the other did like a house
of mourning. The little coffin was borne by eight girls,
who were continually relieved by others running forward
from the procession and taking their places. Behind it
came a straggling company of girls, dressed, as before,
in white and flowers, and including, I should suppose by
their numbers, nearly all the girls between five and fifteen
in the place. They played along on the way, frequently
stopping and running all together to talk to some or to
pick up a flower, and then running on again to overtake
the coffin. There were a few elderly women in common
colors; and a herd of young men and boys, some on foot
and others mounted, followed them, or walked or rode
by their side, frequently interrupting them by jokes and
questions. But the most singular thing of all was, that
two men walked, one on each side of the coffin, carrying
muskets in their hands, which they continually loaded,
and fired into the air. Whether this was to keep off the
evil spirits or not, I do not know. It was the only interpre-
tation that I could put upon it.

As we drew near the Mission, we saw the great gate
thrown open, and the padre standing on the steps, with a
crucifix in his hand. The Mission is a large and deserted-
looking place, the out-buildings going to ruin, and everything giving one the impression of decayed grandeur.
A large stone fountain threw out pure water, from four
mouths, into a basin, before the church door; and we were
on the point of riding up to let our horses drink, when

it occurred to us that it might be consecrated, and we forebore. Just at this moment, the bells set up their harsh, discordant clangor, and the procession moved into the court. I wished to follow, and see the ceremony, but the horse of one of my companions had become frightened, and was tearing off toward the town; and, having thrown his rider, and got one of his hoofs caught in the tackling of the saddle, which had slipped, was fast dragging and ripping it to pieces. Knowing that my shipmate could not speak a word of Spanish, and fearing that he would get into difficulty, I was obliged to leave the ceremony and ride after him. I soon overtook him, trudging along, swearing at the horse, and carrying the remains of the saddle, which he had picked up on the road. Going to the owner of the horse, we made a settlement with him, and found him surprisingly liberal. All parts of the saddle were brought back, and, being capable of repair, he was satisfied with six reáls. We thought it would have been a few dollars. We pointed to the horse, which was now half-way up one of the mountains; but he shook his head, saying, "No importa!" and giving us to understand that he had plenty more.

Having returned to the town, we saw a crowd collected in the square before the principal pulpería, and, riding up, found that all these people—men, women, and children—had been drawn together by a couple of bantam cocks. The cocks were in full tilt, springing into one another, and the people were as eager, laughing and shouting, as though the combatants had been men. There had been a disappointment about the bull; he had broken his bail, and taken himself off, and it was too late to get another, so the people were obliged to put up with a cock-fight. One of the bantams having been knocked in the head, and having an eye put out, gave in, and two monstrous prize-cocks were brought on. These were the object of the whole affair; the bantams having been merely served up as a first course, to collect the people together. Two fellows came into the ring holding the cocks in their arms, and stroking them, and running about on all-fours, encouraging and setting them on. Bets ran high, and, like most other contests, it remained for some time undecided. Both cocks showed great pluck, and fought probably better and longer than their masters would have done. Whether, in the end, it was the white or the red that beat, I do not recollect, but whichever it was, he strutted off with the true veni-vidi-vici look, leaving the other lying panting on his beam-ends.

This matter having been settled, we heard some talk about "caballos" and "carrera," and seeing the people streaming off in one direction, we followed, and came upon a level piece of ground, just out of the town, which was used as a race-course. Here the crowd soon became thick again, the ground was marked off, the judges stationed, and the horses led up to one end. Two fine-looking old gentlemen—Don Carlos and Don Domingo, so called—held the stakes, and all was now ready. We waited some time, during which we could just see the horses twisting round and turning, until, at length, there was a shout along the lines, and on they came, heads stretched out and eyes starting, —working all over, both man and beast. The steeds came by us like a couple of chain shot, —neck and neck; and now we could see nothing but their backs and their hind hoofs flying in the air. As fast as the horses passed, the crowd broke up behind them, and ran to the goal. When we got there, we found the horses returning on a slow walk, having run far beyond the mark, and heard that the long, bony one had come in head and shoulders before the other. The riders were light-built men, had handkerchiefs tied round their heads, and were bare-armed and bare-legged. The horses were noble-looking beasts, not so sleek and combed as our Boston stable horses, but with fine limbs and spirited eyes. After this had been settled, and fully talked over, the crowd scattered again, and flocked back to the town.

Returning to the large pulpería, we heard the violin and guitar screaming and twanging away under the piazza, where they had been all day. As it was now sundown, there began to be some dancing. The Italian sailors danced, and one of our crew exhibited himself in a sort of West India shuffle, much to the amusement of the bystanders, who cried out, "Bravo!" "Otra vez!" and "Vivan los marineros!" but the dancing did not become general, as the women and the "gente de razón" had not yet made their appearance. We wished very much to stay and see the style of dancing; but, although we had had our own way during the day, yet we were, after all, but 'fore-mast Jacks; and, having been ordered to be on the beach by sunset, did not venture to be more than an hour behind the time, so we took our way down. We found the boat just pulling ashore through the breakers, which were running high, there having been a heavy fog outside, which, from some cause or other, always brings on, or precedes, a heavy sea. Liberty-men are privileged from the time they leave the vessel until they step on board again; so we took our places in the stern sheets, and were congratulating ourselves upon getting off dry, when

a great comber broke fore and aft the boat, and wet us
through and through, filling the boat half full of water.
Having lost her buoyancy by the weight of the water, she
dropped heavily into every sea that struck her, and by the
time we had pulled out of the surf into deep water, she
was but just afloat, and we were up to our knees. By the
help of a small bucket and our hats, we bailed her out, got
on board, hoisted the boats, eat [sic] our supper, changed
our clothes, gave (as is usual) the whole history of our
day's adventures to those who had stayed on board, and,
having taken a night-smoke, turned in. Thus ended our
second day's liberty on shore.

On Monday morning, as an offset to our day's sport,
we were all set to work "tarring down" the rigging. Some
got girt-lines up for riding down the stays and back-stays,
and others tarred the shrouds, lifts, &c., laying out on
the yards, and coming down the rigging. We overhauled
our bags, and took out our old tarry trousers and frocks,
which we had used when we tarred down before, and
were all at work in the rigging by sunrise. After breakfast,
we had the satisfaction of seeing the Italian ship's boat
go ashore, filled with men, gayly dressed, as on the day
before, and singing their barcarollas. The Easter holidays
are kept up on shore for three days; and, being a Catholic
vessel, her crew had the advantage of them. For two
successive days, while perched up in the rigging, covered
with tar and engaged in our disagreeable work, we saw
these fellows going ashore in the morning, and coming
off again at night, in high spirits. So much for being Prot-
estants. There's no danger of Catholicism's spreading in
New England, unless the Church cuts down her holidays;
Yankees can't afford the time. American shipmasters get

nearly three weeks' more labor out of their crews, in the course of a year, than the masters of vessels from Catholic countries. As Yankees don't usually keep Christmas, and shipmasters at sea never know when Thanksgiving comes, so Jack has no festival at all.

[…]

This being the spring season, San Pedro, as well as all the other open ports upon the coast, was filled with whales, that had come in to make their annual visit upon soundings. For the first few days that we were here and at Santa Barbara, we watched them with great interest, calling out "There she blows!" every time we saw the spout of one breaking the surface of the water; but they soon became so common that we took little notice of them. They often "broke" very near us, and one thick, foggy night, during a dead calm, while I was standing anchor-watch, one of them rose so near that he struck our cable, and made all surge again. He did not seem to like the encounter much himself, for he sheered off, and spouted at a good distance. We once came very near running one down in the gig, and should probably have been knocked to pieces or thrown skyhigh. We had been on board the little Spanish brig, and were returning, stretching out well at our oars, the little boat going like a swallow; our faces were turned aft (as is always the case in pulling), and the captain, who was steering, was not looking out when, all at once, we heard the spout of a whale directly ahead. "Back water! back water, for your lives!" shouted the captain; and we backed our blades in the water, and brought the boat to in a smother of foam. Turning our heads, we saw a great, rough, hump-backed whale slowly crossing our fore foot, within three or four yards of the boat's stem. Had we not backed water just as we did, we should inevitably have gone smash upon him, striking him with our stem just about amidships. He took no notice of us, but passed slowly on, and dived a few yards beyond us, throwing his tail high in the air. He was so near that we had a perfect view of him, and, as may be supposed, had no desire to see him nearer. He was a disgusting creature, with a skin rough, hairy, and of an iron-gray color. This kind differs much from the sperm, in color and skin, and is said to be fiercer. We saw a few sperm whales; but most of the whales that come upon the coast are fin-backs and hump-backs, which are more difficult to take, and are said not to give oil enough to pay for the trouble. For this reason, whale-ships do not come upon the coast after them. Our captain, together with Captain Nye of the Loriotte, who had been in a whale-ship, thought of making an attempt upon one of them with two boats' crews; but as we had only two harpoons, and no proper lines, they gave it up.

During the months of March, April, and May, these whales appear in great numbers in the open ports of Santa Barbara, San Pedro, &c., and hover off the coast, while a few find their way into the close harbors of San Diego and Monterey. They are all off again before midsummer, and make their appearance on the "off-shore ground." We saw some fine "schools" of sperm whales, which are easily distinguished by their spout, blowing away, a few miles to windward, on our passage to San Juan.

Coasting along on the quiet shore of the Pacific, we came to anchor in twenty fathoms' water, almost out at sea, as it were, and directly abreast of a steep hill which overhung the water, and was twice as high as our royal-mast-head. We had heard much of this place from the Lagoda's crew, who said it was the worst place in California. The shore is rocky, and directly exposed to the southeast, so that vessels are obliged to slip and run for their lives on the first sign of a gale; and late as it was in the season, we got up our slip-rope and gear, though we meant to stay only twenty-four hours. We pulled the agent ashore, and were ordered to wait for him, while he took a circuitous way round the hill to the Mission, which was hidden behind it. We were glad of the opportunity to examine this singular place, and hauling the boat up, and making her well fast, took different directions up and down the beach, to explore it.

San Juan is the only romantic spot on the coast. The country here for several miles is high table-land, running boldly to the shore, and breaking off in a steep cliff, at the foot of which the waters of the Pacific are constantly dashing. For several miles the water washes the very base of the hill, or breaks upon ledges and fragments of rocks which run out into the sea. Just where we landed was a small cove, or bight, which gave us, at high tide, a few square feet of sand-beach between the sea and the bottom of the hill. This was the only landing-place. Directly before us rose the perpendicular height of four or five hundred feet. How we were to get hides down, or goods up, upon the table-land on which the Mission was situated, was more than we could tell. The agent had taken a long circuit, and yet had frequently to jump over breaks, and climb steep places, in the ascent. No animal but a man or a monkey could get up it. However, that was not our lookout; and, knowing that the agent would be gone an hour or more, we strolled about, picking up shells, and following the sea where it tumbled in, roaring and spouting, among the crevices of the great rocks. What a sight, thought I, must this be in a southeaster! The rocks were as large as those of Nahant or Newport, but, to my eye, more grand and broken. Beside, there was a grandeur in everything around, which gave a solemnity to the

scene, a silence and solitariness which affected every part!
Not a human being but ourselves for miles, and no sound
heard but the pulsations of the great Pacific! and the great
steep hill rising like a wall, and cutting us off from all
the world, but the "world of waters"! I separated myself
from the rest, and sat down on a rock, just where the sea
ran in and formed a fine spouting horn. Compared with
the plain, dull sand-beach of the rest of the coast, this
grandeur was as refreshing as a great rock in a weary land.
It was almost the first time that I had been positively
alone—free from the sense that human beings were at
my elbow, if not talking with me—since I had left home.
My better nature returned strong upon me. Everything
was in accordance with my state of feeling, and I expe-
rienced a glow of pleasure at finding that what of poetry
and romance I ever had in me had not been entirely
deadened by the laborious life, with its paltry, vulgar
associations, which I had been leading. Nearly an hour
did I sit, almost lost in the luxury of this entire new scene
of the play in which I had been so long acting, when I
was aroused by the distant shouts of my companions, and
saw that they were collecting together, as the agent had
made his appearance, on his way back to our boat.

San Diego

After we had been a few weeks on shore, and had begun to feel broken into the regularity of our life, its monotony was interrupted by the arrival of two vessels from the windward. We were sitting at dinner in our little room, when we heard the cry of "Sail ho!" This, we had learned, did not always signify a vessel, but was raised whenever a woman was seen coming down from the town, or an ox-cart, or anything unusual, hove in sight upon the road; so we took no notice of it. But it soon became so loud and general from all parts of the beach that we were led to go to the door; and there, sure enough, were two sails coming round the point, and leaning over from the strong northwest wind, which blows down the coast every afternoon. The headmost was a ship, and the other a brig. Everybody was alive on the beach, and all manner of conjectures were abroad. Some said it was the Pilgrim, with the Boston ship, which we were expecting; but we soon saw that the brig was not the Pilgrim, and the ship, with her stump top-gallant-masts and rusty sides, could not be a dandy Boston Indiaman. As they drew nearer, we discovered the high poop, and top-gallant forecastle, and other marks of the Italian ship Rosa, and the brig proved to be the Catalina, which we saw at Santa Barbara, just arrived from Valparaiso. They came to anchor, moored ship, and began discharging hides and tallow. The Rosa had purchased the house occupied by the Lagoda, and the Catalina took the other spare one between ours and the Ayacucho's, so that now each house was occupied, and the beach, for several days, was all animation. The Catalina had several Kanakas on board, who were immediately laid hold of by the others, and carried up to the oven,* where they had a long pow-wow and a smoke. Two Frenchmen, who belonged to the Rosa's crew, came in every evening to see Nicholas; and from them we learned that the Pilgrim was at San Pedro, and was the only vessel from the United States now on the coast. Several of the Italians slept on shore at their hide-house; and there, and at the tent in which the Fazio's crew lived, we had some singing almost every evening. The Italians sang a variety of songs, —barcarollas, provincial airs, &c.; in several of which I recognized parts of our favorite operas and sentimental songs. They often joined in a song, taking the different parts, which produced a fine effect, as many of them had good voices,

---

* Ed. Note: During their time onshore, the Kanakas had taken over a large, abandoned oven, built for bread-baking by the crew of a Russian discovery-ship several years before Dana's arrival. Dana: "It was big enough to hold six or eight men."

and all sang with spirit. One young man, in particular, had a falsetto as clear as a clarionet.

The greater part of the crews of the vessels came ashore every evening, and we passed the time in going about from one house to another, and listening to all manner of languages. The Spanish was the common ground upon which we all met; for every one knew more or less of that. We had now, out of forty or fifty, representatives from almost every nation under the sun, —two Englishmen, three Yankees, two Scotchmen, two Welshmen, one Irishman, three Frenchmen (two of whom were Normans, and the third from Gascony), one Dutchman, one Austrian, two or three Spaniards (from old Spain), half a dozen Spanish-Americans and half-breeds, two native Indians from Chili and the Island of Chiloe, one negro, one mulatto, about twenty Italians, from all parts of Italy, as many more Sandwich-Islanders, one Tahitian, and one Kanaka from the Marquesas Islands.

The night before the vessels were ready to sail, all the Europeans united and had an entertainment at the Rosa's hide-house, and we had songs of every nation and tongue. A German gave us "Ach! mein lieber Augustin!"[;] the three Frenchmen roared through the Marseilles Hymn; the English and Scotchmen gave us "Rule Britannia," and "Wha'll be King but Charlie?"[;] the Italians and Spaniards screamed through some national affairs, for which I was none the wiser; and we three Yankees made an attempt at the "Star-spangled Banner." After these national tributes had been paid, the Austrian gave us a pretty little love-song, and the Frenchmen sang a spirited thing, —"Sentinelle! O prenez garde à vous!"—and then followed the *mélange* which might have been expected.

When I left them, the aguardiente and annisou were pretty well in their heads, and they were all singing and talking at once, and their peculiar national oaths were getting as plenty as pronouns.

The next day, the two vessels got under way for the windward, and left us in quiet possession of the beach.

[...]

We kept up a constant connection with the presidio, and by the close of the summer I had added much to my vocabulary, beside having made the acquaintance of nearly everybody in the place, and acquired some knowledge of the character and habits of the people, as well as of the institutions under which they live.

California was discovered in 1534 by Ximenes, or in 1536 by Cortes, I cannot settle which, and was subsequently visited by many other adventurers, as well as commissioned voyagers of the Spanish crown. It was found to be inhabited by numerous tribes of Indians, and to be in many parts extremely fertile; to which, of course, were added rumors of gold mines, pearl fishery, &c. No sooner was the importance of the country known, than the Jesuits obtained leave to establish themselves in it, to Christianize and enlighten the Indians. They established missions in various parts of the country toward the close of the seventeenth century, and collected the natives about them, baptizing them into the Church, and teaching them the arts of civilized life. To protect the Jesuits in their missions, and at the same time to support the power of the crown over the civilized Indians, two forts were erected and garrisoned, —one at San Diego, and the other at Monterey. These were called presidios, and divided the command of the whole country between them. Presidios have since been established at Santa Barbara, San Francisco, and other places, dividing the country into large districts, each with its presidio, and governed by a commandante. The soldiers, for the most part, married civilized Indians; and thus, in the vicinity of each presidio, sprung up, gradually, small towns. In the course of time, vessels began to come into the ports to trade with the missions and received hides in return; and thus began the great trade of California. Nearly all the cattle in the country belonged to the missions, and they employed their Indians, who became, in fact, their serfs, in tending their vast herds. In the year 1793, when Vancouver visited San Diego, the missions had obtained great wealth and power, and are accused of having depreciated the country with the sovereign, that they might be allowed to retain their possessions. On the expulsion of the Jesuits from the Spanish dominions, the missions passed into the hands of the Franciscans, though without any essential change in their management. Ever since the independence of Mexico, the missions had been going down; until, at last, a law was passed, stripping them of all their possessions, and confining the priests to their spiritual duties, at the same time declaring all the Indians free and independent *Rancheros.* The change in the condition of the Indians was, as may be supposed, only nominal; they are virtually serfs, as much as they ever were. But in the missions the change was complete. The priests have now no power, except in their religious character, and the great possessions of the missions are given over to be preyed upon by the harpies of the civil power, who are sent there in the capacity of *administradores*, to settle up the concerns; and who usually end, in a few years, by making themselves fortunes, and leaving their stewardships worse than they found them. The dynasty of the priests was much more acceptable to the people of the country, and, indeed, to every one concerned with the country, by trade or otherwise, than that of the administradores. The priests were connected permanently to one mission, and felt the necessity of keeping up its credit. Accordingly the debts of the missions were regularly paid, and the people were, in the main, well treated, and attached to those who had spent their whole lives among them. But the administradores are strangers sent from Mexico, having no interest in the country; not identified in any way with their charge, and, for the most part, men of desperate fortunes, —broken-down politicians and soldiers, —whose only object is to retrieve their condition in as short a time as possible. The change had been made but a few years before our arrival upon the coast, yet, in that short time, the trade was much diminished, credit impaired, and the venerable missions were going rapidly to decay.

The external political arrangements remain the same. There are four or more presidios, having under their protection the various missions, and the pueblos, which are towns formed by the civil power and containing no mission or presidio. The most northerly presidio is San Francisco, the next Monterey, the next Santa Barbara, including the mission of the same, San Luis Obispo, and Santa Buenaventura, which is said to be the best mission in the whole country, having fertile soil and rich vineyards. The last, and most southerly, is San Diego, including the mission of the same, San Juan Capistrano, the Pueblo de los Angeles, the largest town in California, with the neighboring mission of San Gabriel. The priests, in spiritual matters, are subject to the Archbishop of Mexico, and in temporal matters to the governor-general, who is the great civil and military head of the country.

The government of the country is an arbitrary democracy, having no common law, and nothing that we should call a judiciary. Their only laws are made and unmade at the caprice of the legislature, and are as variable as the legislature itself. They pass through the form of sending representatives to the congress at Mexico, but as it takes several months to go and return, and there is very little communication between the capital and this distant province, a member usually stays there as permanent member, knowing very well that there will be revolutions at home before he can write and receive an answer; and if another member should be sent, he has only to challenge him, and decide the contested election in that way.

Revolutions are matters of frequent occurrence in California. They are got up by men who are at the foot of the ladder and in desperate circumstances, just as a new political organization may be started by such men in our own country. The only object, of course, is the loaves and fishes; and instead of *caucusing*, paragraphing, libelling, feasting, promising, and lying, they take muskets and bayonets, and, seizing upon the presidio and custom-house, divide the spoils, and declare a new dynasty. As for justice, they know little law but will and fear. A Yankee, who had been naturalized, and become a Catholic, and had married in the country, was sitting in his house at the Pueblo de los Angeles, with his wife and children, when a Mexican, with whom he had had a difficulty, entered the house, and stabbed him to the heart before them all. The murderer was seized by some Yankees who had settled there, and kept in confinement until a statement of the whole affair could be sent to the governor-general. The governor-general refused to do anything about it, and the countrymen of the murdered man, seeing no prospect of justice being administered, gave notice that, if nothing was done, they should try the man themselves. It chanced that, at this time, there was a company of some thirty or forty trappers and hunters from the Western States, with their rifles, who had made their head-quarters at the Pueblo; and these, together with the Americans and Englishmen in the place, who were between twenty and thirty in number, took possession of the town, and, waiting a reasonable time, proceeded to try the man according to the forms in their own country. A judge and jury were appointed, and he was tried, convicted, sentenced to be shot, and carried out before the town blindfolded. The names of all the men were then put into a hat, and each one pledging himself to perform his duty, twelve names were drawn out, and the men took their stations with their rifles, and, firing at the word, laid him dead. He was decently buried, and the place was restored quietly to the proper authorities. A general, with titles enough for an hidalgo, was at San Gabriel, and issued a proclamation as long as the fore-top-bowline, threatening destruction to the rebels, but never stirred from his fort; for forty Kentucky hunters, with their rifles, and a dozen of Yankees and Englishmen, were a match for a whole regiment of hungry, drawling, lazy half-breeds. This affair happened while we were at San Pedro (the port of the Pueblo), and we had the particulars from those who were on the spot. A few months afterwards, another man was murdered on the high-road between the Pueblo and San

Luis Rey by his own wife and a man with whom she ran off. The foreigners pursued and shot them both, according to one story. According to another version, nothing was done about it, as the parties were natives, and a man whom I frequently saw in San Diego was pointed out as the murderer. Perhaps they were two cases, that had got mixed.

When a crime has been committed by Indians, justice, or rather vengeance, is not so tardy. One Sunday afternoon, while I was at San Diego, an Indian was sitting on his horse, when another, with whom he had had some difficulty, came up to him, drew a long knife, and plunged it directly into the horse's heart. The Indian sprang from his falling horse, drew out the knife, and plunged it into the other Indian's breast, over his shoulder, and laid him dead. The fellow was seized at once, clapped into the calabozo, and kept there until an answer could be received from Monterey. A few weeks afterwards I saw the poor wretch, sitting on the bare ground, in front of the calabozo, with his feet chained to a stake, and handcuffs about his wrists. I knew there was very little hope for him. Although the deed was done in hot blood, the horse on which he was sitting being his own, and a favorite with him, yet he was an Indian, and that was enough. In about a week after I saw him, I heard that he had been shot. These few instances will serve to give one a notion of the distribution of justice in California.

In their domestic relations, these people are no better than in their public. The men are thriftless, proud, extravagant, and very much given to gaming; and the women have but little education, and a good deal of beauty, and their morality, of course, is none of the best; yet the instances of infidelity are much less frequent than

against another; and thus something like a balance is obtained. If the women have but little virtue, the jealousy of their husbands is extreme, and their revenge deadly and almost certain. A few inches of cold steel has been the punishment of many an unwary man, who has been guilty, perhaps, of nothing more than indiscretion. The difficulties of the attempt are numerous, and the consequences of discovery fatal, in the better classes. With the unmarried women, too, great watchfulness is used. The main object of the parents is to marry their daughters well, and to this a fair name is necessary. The sharp eyes of a dueña, and the ready weapons of a father or brother, are a protection which the characters of most of them—men and women—render by no means useless; for the very men who would lay down their lives to avenge the dishonor of their own family would risk the same lives to complete the dishonor of another.

Of the poor Indians very little care is taken. The priests, indeed, at the missions, are said to keep them very strictly, and some rules are usually made by the alcaldes to punish their misconduct; yet it all amounts to but little. Indeed, to show the entire want of any sense of morality or domestic duty among them, I have frequently known an Indian to bring his wife, to whom he was lawfully married in the church, down to the beach, and carry her back again, dividing with her the money which she had got from the sailors. If any of the girls were discovered by the alcalde to be open evil-livers, they were whipped, and kept at work sweeping the square of the presidio, and carrying mud and bricks for the buildings; yet a few reáls would generally buy them off. Intemperance, too, is a common vice among the Indians. The Mexicans, on the contrary, are abstemious, and I do not remember ever having seen a Mexican intoxicated.

Such are the people who inhabit a country embracing four or five hundred miles of sea-coast, with several good harbors; with fine forests in the north; the waters filled with fish, and the plains covered with thousands of herds of cattle; blessed with a climate than which there can be no better in the world; free from all manner of diseases, whether epidemic or endemic; and with a soil in which corn yields from seventy to eighty fold. In the hands of an enterprising people, what a country this might be! we are ready to say. Yet how long would a people remain so, in such a country? The Americans (as those from the United States are called) and Englishmen, who are fast filling up the principal towns, and getting the trade into their hands, are indeed more industrious and effective than the Mexicans; yet their children are brought up Mexicans in most respects, and if the "California fever" (laziness) spares the first generation, it is likely to attack the second.

San Francisco, Santa Clara, and San José, December 1835

Our place of destination had been Monterey, but as we were to the northward of it when the wind hauled ahead, we made a fair wind for San Francisco. This large bay, which lies in latitude 37° 58', was discovered by Sir Francis Drake, and by him represented to be (as indeed it is) a magnificent bay, containing several good harbors, great depth of water, and surrounded by a fertile and finely wooded country. About thirty miles from the mouth of the bay, and on the southeast side, is a high point, upon which the Presidio is built. Behind this point is the little harbor, or bight, called Yerba Buena, in which trading-vessels anchor, and, near it, the Mission of Dolores. There was no other habitation on this side of the Bay, except a shanty of rough boards put up by a man named Richardson, who was doing a little trading between the vessels and the Indians.* Here, at anchor, and the only vessel, was a brig under Russian colors, from Sitka, in Russian America, which had come down to winter, and to take in a supply of tallow and grain, great quantities of which later article are raised in the Missions at the head of the bay. The second day after our arrival we went on board the brig, it being Sunday, as a matter of curiosity; and there was enough there to gratify it. Though no larger than the Pilgrim, she had five or six officers, and a crew of between twenty and thirty; and such a stupid and greasy-looking set, I never saw before. Although it was quite comfortable weather and we had nothing on but straw hats, shirts, and duck trousers, and were bare-footed, they had, every man of them, doubled-soled boots, coming up to the knees, and well greased; thick woollen trousers, frocks, waistcoats, pea-jackets, woollen caps, and everything in true Nova Zembla rig; and in the warmest days they made no change. The clothing of one of these men would weigh nearly as much as that of half our crew. They had brutish faces, looked like the antipodes of sailors, and apparently dealt in nothing but grease. They lived upon grease; eat it, drank it, slept in the midst of it, and their clothes were covered with it. To a Russian, grease is the greatest luxury. They looked with greedy eyes upon the tallow-bags as they were taken into the vessel, and, no doubt, would have eaten one up whole, had not the officer kept watch over it. The grease appeared to fill their pores, and to come out

---

* The next year Richardson built a one-story adobe house on the same spot, which was long afterwards known as the oldest house in the great city of San Francisco.

in their hair and on their faces. It seems as if it were this saturation which makes them stand cold and rain so well. If they were to go into a warm climate, they would melt and die of the scurvy.

The vessel was no better than the crew. Everything was in the oldest and most inconvenient fashion possible: running trusses and lifts on the yards, and large hawser cables, coiled all over the decks, and served and parcelled in all directions. The topmasts, top-gallant-masts, and studding-sail booms were nearly black for want of scraping, and the decks would have turned the stomach of a man-of-war's-man. The galley was down in the forecastle; and there the crew lived, in the midst of the steam and grease of the cooking, in a place as hot as an oven, and apparently never cleaned out. Five minutes in the forecastle was enough for us, and we were glad to get into the open air. We made some trade with them, buying Indian curiosities, of which they had a great number; such as bead-work, feathers of birds, fur moccasons, &c. I purchased a large robe, made of the skins of some animals, dried and sewed nicely together, and covered all over on the outside with thick downy feathers, taken from the breasts of various birds, and arranged with their different colors so as to make a brilliant show.

A few days after our arrival the rainy season set in, and for three weeks it rained almost every hour, without cessation. This was bad for our trade, for the collecting of hides is managed differently in this port from what it is in any other on the coast. The Mission of Dolores, near the anchorage, has no trade at all; but those of San José, Santa Clara, and others situated on the large creeks or rivers which run into the bay, and distant between fifteen and forty miles from the anchorage, do a greater business in hides than any in California. Large boats, or launches, manned by Indians, and capable of carrying from five to six hundred hides apiece, are attached to the Missions, and sent down to the vessels with hides, to bring away goods in return. Some of the crews of the vessels are obliged to go and come in the boats, to look out for the hides and goods. These are favorite expeditions with the sailors in fine weather; but now, to be gone three or four days, in open boats, in constant rain, without any shelter, and with cold food, was hard service. Two of our men went up to Santa Clara in one of these boats, and were gone three days, during all which time they had a constant rain, and did not sleep a wink, but passed three long nights walking fore and aft the boat, in the open air. When they got on board they were completely exhausted, and took a watch below of twelve hours. All the hides, too, that came down in the boats were soaked with water, and unfit to put below, so that we were obliged to trice them up to dry, in the intervals of sunshine or wind, upon all parts of the vessel. We got up tricing-lines from the jib-boom-end to each arm of the fore yard, and thence to the main and cross-jack yard-arms. Between the tops, too, and the mast-heads, from the fore to the main swifters, and thence to the mizzen rigging, and in all directions athwartships, tricing-lines were run, and strung with hides. The head stays and guys, and the spritsail yard were lined, and, having still more, we got out the swinging-booms, and strung them and the forward and after guys with hides. The rail, fore and aft, the windlass, capstan, the sides of the ship, and every vacant place on deck, were covered with wet hides, on the least sign of an interval

for drying. Our ship was nothing but a mass of hides, from the cat-harpins to the water's edge, and from the jib-boom-end to the taffrail.

One cold, rainy evening, about eight o'clock, I received orders to get ready to start for San José at four the next morning, in one of these Indian boats, with four days' provisions. I got my oil-cloth clothes, southwester, and thick boots ready, and turned into my hammock early, determined to get some sleep in advance, as the boat was to be alongside before daybreak. I slept on till all hands were called in the morning; for, fortunately for me, the Indians, intentionally, or from mistaking their orders, had gone off alone in the night, and were far out of sight. Thus I escaped three or four days of very uncomfortable service.

Four of our men, a few days afterwards, went up in one of the quarter-boats to Santa Clara, to carry the agent, and remained out all night in a drenching rain, in the small boat, in which there was not room for them to turn round; the agent having gone up to the Mission and left the men to their fate, making no provision for their accommodation, and not even sending them anything to eat. After this they had to pull thirty miles, and when they got on board were so stiff that they could not come up the gangway ladder. This filled up the measure of the agent's unpopularity, and never after this could he get anything done for him by the crew; and many a delay and vexation, and many a good ducking in the surf, did he get to pay up old scores, or "square the yards with the bloody quill-driver."

Having collected nearly all the hides that were to be procured, we began our preparations for taking in a supply of wood and water, for both of which San Francisco is the best place on the coast. A small island, about two leagues from the anchorage, called by us "Wood Island," and by the Mexicans "Isla de los Angeles," was covered with trees to the water's edge; and to this two of our crew, who were Kennebec men, and could handle an axe like a plaything, were sent every morning to cut wood, with two boys to pile it up for them. In about a week they had cut enough to last us a year, and the third mate, with myself and three others, were sent over in a large, schooner-rigged, open launch, which we had hired of the Mission, to take in the wood, and bring it to the ship. We left the ship about noon, but owing to a strong head wind, and a tide which here runs four or five knots, did not get into the harbor, formed by two points of the island, where the boats lie, until sundown. No sooner had we come-to, than a strong southeaster, which had been threatening us all day, set in, with heavy rain and a chilly air. We were in rather a bad situation: an open boat, a heavy rain, and a long night; for in winter, in this latitude, it was dark nearly fifteen hours. Taking a small skiff which we had brought with us, we went ashore, but discovered no shelter, for everything was open to the rain; and, collecting a little wood, which we found by lifting up the leaves and brush, and a few mussels, we put aboard again, and made the best preparations in our power for passing the night. We unbent the mainsail, and formed an awning with it over the after part of the boat, made a bed of wet logs of wood, and, with our jackets on, lay down, about six o'clock, to sleep. Finding the rain running down upon us, and our jackets getting wet through, and the rough, knotty logs rather indifferent couches, we turned out; and, taking an iron pan which we brought with us, we wiped it out dry, put some stones around it, cut the wet bark from some sticks, and, striking a light, made a small fire in the pan. Keeping some sticks near to dry, and covering the whole over with a roof of boards, we kept up a small fire, by which we cooked our mussels, and ate them, rather for an occupation than from hunger. Still it was not ten o'clock, and the night was long before us, when one of the party produced an old pack of Spanish cards from his monkey-jacket pocket, which we hailed as a great windfall; and, keeping a dim, flickering light by our fagots, we played game after game, till one or two o'clock, when, becoming really tired, we went to our logs again, one sitting up at a time, in turn, to keep watch over the fire. Toward morning the rain ceased, and the air became sensibly colder, so that we found sleep impossible, and sat up, watching for daybreak. No sooner was it light than we went ashore, and began our preparations for loading our vessel. We were not mistaken in the coldness of the weather, for a white frost was on the ground, and—a thing we had never seen before in California—one or two little puddles of fresh water were skimmed over with a thin coat of ice. In this state of the weather, and before sunrise, in the gray of the morning, we had to wade off, nearly up to our hips in water, to load the skiff with the wood by armfuls. The third mate remained on board the launch, two more men stayed in the skiff to load and manage it, and all the water-work, as usual, fell upon the two youngest of us; and there we were with frost on the ground, wading forward and back, from the beach to the boat, with armfuls of wood, barefooted, and our trousers rolled up. When the skiff went off with her load, we could only keep our feet from freezing by racing up and down the beach on the hard sand, as fast as we could go. We were all day at this work, and toward sundown, having loaded the vessel as deep as she would bear, we hove up our anchor and made sail, beating out of the bay. No sooner had we got into the large bay than we found a strong tide setting us out to seaward, a thick fog which prevented our seeing the ship, and a breeze too light to set us against the tide, for we were as deep as a sand-barge. By the utmost exertions, we saved ourselves from being carried out to sea, and were glad to reach the leewardmost point of the island, where we came-to, and prepared to pass another night more uncomfortable than the first, for we were loaded up to the gunwale, and had only a choice among logs and sticks for a resting-place. The next morning we made sail at slack water, with a fair wind, and got on board by eleven o'clock, when all hands were turned-to to unload and stow away the wood, which took till night.

Having now taken in all our wood, the next morning a water-party was ordered off with all the casks. From this we escaped, having had a pretty good siege with the wooding. The water-party were gone three days, during which time they narrowly escaped being carried out to sea, and passed one day on an island, where one of them shot a deer, great numbers of which overrun the islands and hills of San Francisco Bay.

While not off on these wood and water parties, or up the rivers to the Missions, we had easy times on board the ship. We were moored, stem and stern, within a cable's length of the shore, safe from southeasters, and with little boating to do; and, as it rained nearly all the time, awnings were put over the hatchways, and all hands sent down between decks, where we were at work, day after day, picking oakum, until we got enough to calk the ship all over, and to last the whole voyage. Then we made a whole suit of gaskets for the voyage home, a pair of wheel-ropes from strips of green hide, great quantities of spun-yarn, and everything else that could be made between decks. It being now midwinter and in high latitude, the nights were very long, so that we were not turned-to until seven in the morning, and were obliged to knock off at five in the evening, when we got supper; which gave us nearly three hours before eight bells, at which time the watch was set.

As we had now been about a year on the coast, it was time to think of the voyage home; and, knowing that the last two or three months of our stay would be very busy ones, and that we should never have so good an opportunity to work for ourselves as the present, we all employed our evenings in making clothes for the passage home, and more especially for Cape Horn. As soon as supper was over and the kids cleared away, and each man had taken his smoke, we seated ourselves on our chests round the lamp, which swung from a beam, and went to work each in his own way, some making hats, others trousers, others jackets, &c., &c., and no one was idle. The boys who could not sew well enough to make their own clothes laid up grass into sinnet for the men, who sewed for them in return. Several of us clubbed together and bought a large piece of twilled cotton, which we made into trousers and jackets, and, giving them several coats of linseed oil, laid them by for Cape Horn. I also sewed and covered a tarpaulin hat, thick and strong enough to sit upon, and made myself a complete suit of flannel underclothing for bad weather. Those who had no southwester caps made them; and several of the crew got up for themselves tarpaulin jackets and trousers, lined on the inside with flannel. Industry was the order of the day, and every one did something for himself; for we knew that as the season advanced, and we went further south, we should have no evenings to work in.

Friday, December 25th. This day was Christmas; and, as it rained all day long, and there were no hides to take in, and nothing especial to do, the captain gave us a holiday (the first we had had, except Sundays, since leaving Boston), and plum-duff for dinner. The Russian brig, following the Old Style, had celebrated their Christmas eleven days before, when they had a grand blow-out, and (as our men said) drank, in the forecastle, a barrel of gin, ate up a bag of tallow, and made a soup of the skin.

Sunday, December 27th. We had now finished all our business at this port, and, it being Sunday, we unmoored ship and got under way, firing a salute to the Russian brig, and another to the presidio, which were both answered. The commandante of the presidio, Don Guadalupe Vallejo, a young man, and the most popular, among the Americans and English, of any man in California, was on board when we got under way. He spoke English very well, and was suspected of being favorably inclined to foreigners.

We sailed down this magnificent bay with a light wind, the tide, which was running out, carrying us at the rate of four or five knots. It was a fine day; the first of entire sunshine we had had for more than a month. We passed directly under the high cliff on which the presidio is built, and stood into the middle of the bay, from whence we could see small bays making up into the interior, large and beautifully wooded islands, and the mouths of several small rivers. If California ever becomes a prosperous country, this bay will be the centre of its prosperity. The abundance of wood and water; the extreme fertility of its shores; the excellence of its climate, which is as near to being perfect as any in the world; and its facilities for navigation, affording the best anchoring-grounds in the whole western coast of America, —all fit it for a place of great importance.

The tide leaving us, we came to anchor near the mouth of the bay, under a high and beautifully sloping hill, upon which herds of hundreds and hundreds of red deer, and the stag, with his high branching antlers, were bounding about, looking at us for a moment, and then starting off, affrighted at the noises which we made for the purpose of seeing the variety of their beautiful attitudes and motions. At midnight, the tide having turned, we hove up our anchor and stood out of the bay, with a fine starry heaven above us, —the first we had seen for many weeks. Before the light northerly winds, which blow here with the regularity of trades, we worked slowly along, and made Point Año Nuevo, the northerly point of the Bay of Monterey, on Monday afternoon. We spoke, going in, the brig Diana, of the Sandwich Islands, from the Northwest Coast, last from Sitka. She was off the point at the same time with us, but did not get in to the anchoring-ground until an hour or two after us. It was ten o'clock on Tuesday morning when we came to anchor. Monterey looked just as it did when I saw it last, which was eleven months before, in the brig Pilgrim. The pretty lawn on which it stands, as green as sun and rain could make it; the pine wood on the south; the small river on the north side; the adobe houses, with their white walls and red-tiled roofs, dotted about on the green; the low, white presidio, with its soiled tri-colored flag flying, and the discordant din of drums and trumpets of the noon parade, —all brought up the scene we had witnessed here with so much pleasure nearly a year before, when coming from a long voyage, and from our unprepossessing reception at Santa Barbara. It seemed almost like coming to a home.

Santa Barbara, January–March 1836

Wednesday, *January 6th*. Set sail from Monterey, with a number of Mexicans as passengers, and shaped our course for Santa Barbara. The Diana went out of the bay in company with us, but parted from us off Point Pinos, being bound to the Sandwich Islands. We had a smacking breeze for several hours, and went along at a great rate until night, when it died away, as usual, and the land-breeze set in, which brought us upon a taut bowline. Among our passengers was a young man who was a good representation of a decayed gentleman. He reminded me much of some of the characters in *Gil Blas*.* He was of the aristocracy of the country, his family being of pure Spanish blood, and once of considerable importance in Mexico. His father had been governor of the province, and, having amassed

---

* Ed. Note: A French novel (1715–1735) by Alain-René Lesage.

a large property, settled at San Diego, where he built a large house with a court-yard in front, kept a retinue of Indians, and set up for the grandee of that part of the country. His son was sent to Mexico, where he received an education, and went into the first society of the capital. Misfortune, extravagance, and the want of any manner of getting interest on money, soon ate the estate up, and Don Juan Bandini returned from Mexico accomplished, poor, and proud, and without any office or occupation, to lead the life of most young men of the better families, — dissipated and extravagant when the means are at hand; ambitious at heart, and impotent in act; often pinched for bread; keeping up an appearance of style, when their poverty is known to each half-naked Indian boy in the street, and standing in dread of every small trader and shopkeeper in the place. He had a slight and elegant figure, moved gracefully, danced and waltzed beautifully, spoke good Castilian, with a pleasant and refined voice and accent, and had, throughout, the bearing of a man of birth and figure. Yet here he was, with his passage given him (as I afterwards learned), for he had not the means of paying for it, and living upon the charity of our agent. He was polite to every one, spoke to the sailors, and gave four reáls—I dare say the last he had in his pocket—to the steward, who waited upon him. I could not but feel a pity for him, especially when I saw him by the side of his fellow-passenger and townsman, a fat, coarse, vulgar, pretentious fellow of a Yankee trader, who had made money in San Diego, and was eating out the vitals of the Bandinis, fattening upon their extravagance, grinding them in their poverty; having mortgages on their lands, forestalling their cattle, and already making an inroad upon their jewels, which were their last hope.

Don Juan had with him a retainer, who was as much like many of the characters in *Gil Blas* as his master. He called himself a private secretary, though there was no writing for him to do, and he lived in the steerage with the carpenter and sailmaker. He was certainly a character; could read and write well; spoke good Spanish; had been over the greater part of Spanish America, and lived in every possible situation, and served in every conceivable capacity, though generally in that of confidential servant to some man of figure. I cultivated this man's acquaintance, and during the five weeks that he was with us, — for he remained on board until we arrived at San Diego, —I gained a greater knowledge of the state of political parties in Mexico, and the habits and affairs of the different classes of society, than I could have learned from almost any one else. He took great pains in correcting my Spanish, and supplying me with colloquial phrases, and common terms and exclamations, in speaking. He lent me a file of late newspapers from the city of Mexico, which were full of the triumphal reception of Santa Ana, who had just returned from Tampico after a victory, and with the preparations for his expedition against the Texans. "Viva Santa Ana!" was the byword everywhere, and it had even reached California, though there were still many here, among whom was Don Juan Bandini, who were opposed to his government, and intriguing to bring in Bustamente. Santa Ana, they said, was for breaking down the Missions; or, as they termed it, "Santa Ana no quiere religion." Yet I had no doubt that the office of administrador of San Diego would reconcile Don Juan to any dynasty, and any state of the church. In these papers, too, I found scraps of American and English news; but which was so unconnected, and I was so ignorant of everything preceding them for eighteen months past, that they only awakened a curiosity which they could not satisfy. One article spoke of Taney as Justicia Mayor de los Estados Unidos, (what had become of Marshall? was he dead, or banished?) and another made known, by news received from Vera Cruz, that "El Vizconde Melbourne" had returned to the office of "primer ministro," in place of Sir Roberto Peel. (Sir Robert Peel had been minister, then? and where were Earl Grey and the Duke of Wellington?) Here were the outlines of grand political overturns, the filling up of which I was left to imagine at my leisure.

[...]

Sunday, January 10th. Arrived at Santa Barbara, and on the following Wednesday slipped our cable and went to sea, on account of a southeaster. Returned to our anchorage the next day. We were the only vessel in the port. The Pilgrim had passed through the Canal and hove-to off the town, nearly six weeks before, on her passage down from Monterey, and was now at the leeward. She heard here of our safe arrival at San Francisco.

Great preparations were making on shore for the marriage of our agent, who was to marry Doña Anita de la Guerra de Noriego y Corillo, youngest daughter of Don Antonio Noriego, the grandee of the place, and the head of the first family in California. Our steward was ashore three days, making pastry and cake, and some of the best of our stores were sent off with him. On the day appointed for the wedding, we took the captain ashore in the gig, and had orders to come for him at night, with

leave to go up to the house and see the fandango. Returning on board, we found preparations making for a salute.
Our guns were loaded and run out, men appointed to
each, cartridges served out, matches lighted, and all the
flags ready to be run up. I took my place at the starboard
after gun, and we all waited for the signal from on shore.
At ten o'clock the bride went up with her sister to the
confessional, dressed in deep black. Nearly an hour
intervened, when the great doors of the Mission church
opened, the bells rang out a loud, discordant peal, the
private signal for us was run up by the captain ashore, the
bride, dressed in complete white, came out of the church
with the bridegroom, followed by a long procession. Just
as she stepped from the church door, a small white cloud
issued from the bows of our ship, which was full in sight,
the loud report echoed among the surrounding hills and
over the bay, and instantly the ship was dressed in flags
and pennants from stem to stern. Twenty-three guns
followed in regular succession, with an interval of fifteen
seconds between each, when the cloud blew off, and our
ship lay dressed in her colors all day. At sundown another
salute of the same number of guns was fired, and all the
flags run down. This we thought was pretty well—a gun
every fifteen seconds—for a merchantman with only four
guns and a dozen or twenty men.

After supper, the gig's crew were called, and we rowed
ashore, dressed in our uniform, beached the boat, and
went up to the fandango. The bride's father's house
was the principal one in the place, with a large court in
front, upon which a tent was built, capable of containing several hundred people. As we drew near, we heard
the accustomed sound of violins and guitars, and saw a

great motion of the people within. Going in, we found nearly all the people of the town—men, women, and children—collected and crowded together, leaving barely room for the dancers; for on these occasions no invitations are given, but every one is expected to come, though there is always a private entertainment within the house for particular friends. The old women sat down in rows, clapping their hands to the music, and applauding the young ones. The music was lively, and among the tunes we recognized several of our popular airs, which we, without doubt, have taken from the Spanish. In the dancing I was much disappointed. The women stood upright, with their hands down by their sides, their eyes fixed upon the ground before them, and slided about without any perceptible means of motion; for their feet were invisible, the hem of their dresses forming a circle about them, reaching to the ground. They looked as grave as though they were going through some religious ceremony, their faces as little excited as their limbs; and on the whole, instead of the spirited, fascinating Spanish dances which I had expected, I found the Californian fandango, on the part of the women at least, a lifeless affair. The men did better. They danced with grace and spirit, moving in circles round their nearly stationary partners, and showing their figures to advantage.

A great deal was said about our friend Don Juan Bandini, and when he did appear, which was toward the close of the evening, he certainly gave us the most graceful dancing that I had ever seen. He was dressed in white pantaloons, neatly made, a short jacket of dark silk, gayly figured, white stockings and thin morocco slippers upon his very small feet. His slight and graceful figure was well

adapted to dancing, and he moved about with the grace
and daintiness of a young fawn. An occasional touch of
the toe to the ground seemed all that was necessary to
give him a long interval of motion in the air. At the same
time he was not fantastic or flourishing, but appeared
to be rather repressing a strong tendency to motion. He
was loudly applauded, and danced frequently toward
the close of the evening. After the supper, the waltzing
began, which was confined to a very few of the "gente de
razón," and was considered a high accomplishment, and
a mark of aristocracy. Here, too, Don Juan figured greatly,
waltzing with the sister of the bride (Doña Angustias, a
handsome woman and a general favorite) in a variety of
beautiful figures, which lasted as much as half an hour,
no one else taking the floor. They were repeatedly and
loudly applauded, the old men and women jumping out
of their seats in admiration, and the young people waving
their hats and handkerchiefs. The great amusement of
the evening—owing to its being the Carnival—was the
breaking of eggs filled with cologne, or other essences,
upon the heads of the company. The women bring a great
number of these secretly about them, and the amusement
is to break one upon the head of a gentleman when his
back is turned. He is bound in gallantry to find out the
lady and return the compliment, though it must not be
done if the person sees you. A tall, stately Don, with
immense gray whiskers, and a look of great importance,
was standing before me, when I felt a light hand on my
shoulder, and, turning round, saw Doña Angustias (whom
we all knew, as she had been up to Monterey, and down
again, in the Alert), with her finger upon her lip, motion-
ing me gently aside. I stepped back a little, when she went

up behind the Don, and with one hand knocked off his huge *sombrero*, and at the same instant, with the other, broke the egg upon his head, and, springing behind me, was out of sight in a moment. The Don turned slowly round, the cologne running down his face and over his clothes, and a loud laugh breaking out from every quarter. He looked round in vain for some time, until the direction of so many laughing eyes showed him the fair offender. She was his niece, and a great favorite with him, so old Don Domingo had to join in the laugh. A great many such tricks were played, and many a war of sharp manoeuvering was carried on between couples of the younger people, and at every successful exploit a general laugh was raised.

Another of their games I was for some time at a loss about. A pretty young girl was dancing, named—after what would appear to us an almost sacrilegious custom of the country—Espíritu Santo, when a young man went behind her and placed his hat directly upon her head, letting it fall down over her eyes, and sprang back among the crowd. She danced for some time with the hat on, when she threw it off, which called forth a general shout, and the young man was obliged to go out upon the floor and pick it up. Some of the ladies, upon whose heads hats had been placed, threw them off at once, and a few kept them on throughout the dance, and took them off at the end, and held them out in their hands, when the owner stepped out, bowed, and took it from them. I soon began to suspect the meaning of the thing, and was afterwards told that it was a compliment, and an offer to become the lady's gallant for the rest of the evening, and to wait upon her home. If the hat was thrown off, the offer was refused, and the gentleman was obliged to pick up his hat amid a general laugh. Much amusement was caused sometimes by gentlemen putting hats on the ladies' heads, without permitting them to see whom it was done by. This obliged them to throw them off, or keep them on at a venture, and when they came to discover the owner the laugh was turned upon one or the other.

The captain sent for us about ten o'clock, and we went aboard in high spirits, having enjoyed the new scene much, and were of great importance among the crew, from having so much to tell, and from the prospect of going every night until it was over; for these fandangos generally last three days. The next day, two of us were sent up to the town, and took care to come back by way of Señor Noriego's, and take a look into the booth. The musicians were again there, upon their platform, scraping and twanging away, and a few people, apparently of the lower classes, were dancing. The dancing is kept up, at intervals, throughout the day, but the crowd, the spirit, and the *élite* come in at night. The next night, which was the last, we went ashore in the same manner, until we got almost tired of the monotonous twang of the instruments, the drawling sounds which the women kept up, as an accompaniment, and the slapping of the hands in time with the music, in place of castanets. We found ourselves as great objects of attention as any persons or anything at the place. Our sailor dresses—and we took great pains to have them neat and ship-shape—were much admired, and we were invited, from every quarter, to give them an American dance; but after the ridiculous figure some of our countrymen cut in dancing after the Mexicans, we thought it best to leave it to their imaginations.

Our agent, with a tight, black, swallow-tailed coat just imported from Boston, a high stiff cravat, looking as if he had been pinned and skewered, with only his feet and hands left free, took the floor just after Bandini, and we thought they had had enough of Yankee grace.

The last night they kept it up in great style, and were getting into a high-go, when the captain called us off to go aboard, for, it being southeaster season, he was afraid to remain on shore long; and it was well he did not, for that night we slipped our cables, as a crowner to our fun ashore, and stood off before a southeaster, which lasted twelve hours, and returned to our anchorage the next day.

[...]

Saturday, March 5th. This was an important day in our almanac, for it was on this day that we were first assured that our voyage was really drawing to a close. The captain gave orders to have the ship ready for getting under way; and observed that there was a good breeze to take us down to San Pedro. Then we were not going up to windward. Thus much was certain, and was soon known fore and aft; and when we went in the gig to take him off, he shook hands with the people on the beach, and said that he did not expect to see Santa Barbara again. This settled the matter, and sent a thrill of pleasure through the heart of every one in the boat. We pulled off with a will, saying to ourselves (I can speak for myself at least), "Good by, Santa Barbara! This is the last pull here! No more duckings in your breakers, and slipping from your cursed southeasters!" The news was soon known aboard, and put life into everything when we were getting under way. Each one was taking his last look at the Mission, the town, the breakers on the beach, and swearing that

no money would make him ship to see them again; and
when all hands tallied on to the cat-fall, the chorus of
"Time for us to go!" was raised for the first time, and
joined in, with full swing, by everybody. One would have
thought we were on our voyage home, so near did it seem
to us, though there were yet three months for us on the
coast.

[...]

Two days brought us to San Pedro, and two days more
(to our no small joy) gave us our last view of that place,
which was universally called the hell of California, and
seemed designed in every way for the wear and tear of
sailors. Not even the last view could bring out one feeling
of regret. No thanks, thought I, as we left the hated
shores in the distance, for the hours I have walked over
your stones barefooted, with hides on my head, —for the
burdens I have carried up your steep, muddy hill, —for
the duckings in your surf; and for the long days and
longer nights passed on your desolate hill, watching piles
of hides, hearing the sharp bark of your eternal coyotes,
and the dismal hooting of your owls.

As I bade good by to each successive place, I felt as
though one link after another were struck from the
chain of my servitude. Having kept close in shore for the
land-breeze, we passed the Mission of San Juan Capistrano the same night, and saw distinctly, by the bright
moonlight, the cliff which I had gone down by a pair of
halyards in search of a few paltry hides. "Forsan et hæc
olim,"* thought I, and took my last look of that place too.
And on the next morning we were under the high point

---

* Ed. Note: "Perhaps one day it will give us pleasure."

of San Diego. The flood tide took us swiftly in, and we came-to opposite our hide-house, and prepared to get everything in trim for a long stay. This was our last port. Here we were to discharge everything from the ship, clean her out, smoke her, take in our hides, wood, and water, and set sail for Boston. While all this was doing, we were to lie still in one place, the port a safe one, and no fear of southeasters. Accordingly, having picked out a good berth in the stream, with a smooth beach opposite for a landing-place, and within two cables' length of our hide-house, we moored ship, unbent the sails, sent down the top-gallant-yards and the studding-sail booms, and housed the top-gallant-masts. The boats were then hove out and all the sails, the spare spars, the stores, the rigging not rove, and, in fact, everything which was not in daily use, sent ashore, and stowed away in the house. Then went our hides and horns, and we left hardly anything in the ship but her ballast, and this we made preparations to heave out the next day. At night, after we had knocked off, and were sitting round in the forecastle, smoking and talking, and taking sailor's pleasure, we congratulated ourselves upon being in that situation in which we had wished ourselves every time we had come into San Diego. "If we were only here for the last time," we had often said, "with our top-gallant-masts housed and our sails unbent!"—and now we had our wish. Six weeks, or two months, of the hardest work we had yet seen, but not the most disagreeable or trying, was before us, and then—"Good by to California!"

A California Legacy Book

Santa Clara University and Heyday Books are pleased to publish the California Legacy series, vibrant and relevant writings drawn from California's past and present.

Santa Clara University—founded in 1851 on the site of the eighth of California's original twenty-one missions—is the oldest institution of higher learning in the state. A Jesuit institution, it is particularly aware of its contribution to California's cultural heritage and its responsibility to preserve and celebrate that heritage.

Heyday Books, founded in 1974, specializes in critically acclaimed books on California literature, history, natural history, and ethnic studies.

Books in the California Legacy series appear as anthologies, single author collections, reprints of important books, and original works. Taken together, these volumes bring readers a new perspective on California's cultural life, a perspective that honors diversity and finds great pleasure in the eloquence of human expression.

Series editor: Terry Beers
Publisher: Malcolm Margolin
Advisory committee: Stephen Becker, William Deverell, Charles Faulhaber, David Fine, Steven Gilbar, Ron Hansen, Gerald Haslam, Robert Hass, Jack Hicks, Timothy Hodson, Jeanne Wakatsuki Houston, Maxine Hong Kingston, Frank LaPena, Ursula K. Le Guin, Jeff Lustig, Ishmael Reed, Alan Rosenus, Robert Senkewicz, Gary Snyder, Kevin Starr, Richard Walker, Alice Waters, Jennifer Watts, Al Young.

Thanks to the English Department at Santa Clara University and to Regis McKenna for their support of the California Legacy series.

For more on California Legacy titles, events, or other information, please visit www.californialegacy.org.

Other California Legacy Books

The Anza Trail and the Settling of California *Vladimir Guerrero*

California: A Study of American Character *Josiah Royce*

Death Valley in '49 *William Lewis Manly*

Eldorado: Adventures in the Path of Empire *Bayard Taylor*

Gunfight at Mussel Slough: Evolution of a Western Myth
Edited by Terry Beers

The Journey of the Flame
Walter Nordhoff with a Foreword by Rebecca Solnit

Lands of Promise and Despair: Chronicles of Early California, 1535-1846
Edited by Rose Marie Beebe and Robert M. Senkewicz

Life in a California Mission: Monterey in 1786
Jean François de la Pérouse, Introduction by Malcolm Margolin

Mark Twain's San Francisco
Edited with a New Introduction by Bernard Taper

Mountains and Molehills
Frank Maryatt, Foreword by Robert J. Chandler

The Shirley Letters: From the California Mines, 1851-1852
Louise Amelia Knapp Smith Clappe

Under the Fifth Sun: Latino Literature in California
Edited by Rick Heide

Unfolding Beauty: Celebrating California's Landscapes
Edited with an Introduction by Terry Beers

Unsettling the West: Eliza Farnham and Georgiana Bruce Kirby in
Frontier California *JoAnn Levy*

HEYDAY INSTITUTE

Since its founding in 1974, Heyday Books has occupied a unique niche in the publishing world, specializing in books that foster an understanding of the history, literature, art, environment, social issues, and culture of California and the West. We are a 501(c)(3) nonprofit organization based in Berkeley, California, serving a wide range of people and audiences.

We are grateful for the generous funding we've received for our publications and programs during the past year from foundations and more than three hundred and fifty individual donors. Major supporters include:

Anonymous; Audubon California; Judith and Phillip Auth; Barona Band of Mission Indians; B.C.W. Trust III; S. D. Bechtel, Jr. Foundation; Barbara and Fred Berensmeier; Berkeley Civic Arts Program; Joan Berman; Black Oak Casino; Book Club of California; Peter and Mimi Buckley; Buena Vista Rancheria; Lewis and Sheana Butler; Butler Koshland Fund; California State Automobile Association; California State Coastal Conservancy; California State Library; Joanne Campbell; Candelaria Fund; John and Nancy Cassidy Family Foundation, through Silicon Valley Community Foundation; Malcolm Cravens Foundation; Creative Work Fund; Columbia Foundation; Colusa Indian Community Council; The Community Action Fund; Community Futures Collective; Compton Foundation, Inc.; Lawrence Crooks; Ida Rae Egli; Elk Valley Rancheria; Donald and Janice Elliott, in honor of David Elliott, through Silicon Valley Community Foundation; Evergreen Foundation; Federated Indians of Graton Rancheria; Fleishhacker Foundation; Wallace Alexander Gerbode Foundation; Richard & Rhoda Goldman Fund; Ben Graber, in honor of Sandy Graber; Evelyn & Walter Haas, Jr. Fund; Walter & Elise Haas Fund; James and Coke Hallowell; Cheryl Hinton; Hopland Band of Pomo Indians; James Irvine Foundation; Mehdi Kashef; Marty and Pamela Krasney; LEF Foundation; Michael McCone; Middletown Rancheria Tribal Council; Morongo Band of Mission Indians; National Endowment for the Arts; National Park Service;

Pease Family Fund, in honor of Bruce Kelley; Philanthropic Ventures Foundation; Resources Legacy Fund; River Rock Casino; Robinson Rancheria Citizens Council; Alan Rosenus; San Francisco Foundation; Seaver Institute; Skirball Foundation; Deborah Sanchez; William Saroyan Foundation; Contee and Maggie Seely; Sandy Cold Shapero; Stanford University; Jim Swinerton; Swinerton Family Fund; Taproot Foundation; Thendara Foundation; Marion Weber; Albert and Susan Wells; Peter Booth Wiley; Dean Witter Foundation; and Dolores Zohrab Liebmann Fund.

For more information about Heyday Institute, our publications and programs, please visit our website at www.heydaybooks.com.

Heyday Books is committed to preserving ancient forests and natural resources. We elected to print this title on 30% post consumer recycled paper, processed chlorine free. As a result, for this printing, we have saved:

3 Trees (40′ tall and 6-8″ diameter)
1 Million BTUs of Total Energy
240 Pounds of Greenhouse Gases
1,155 Gallons of Wastewater
80 Pounds of Solid Waste

Heyday Books made this paper choice because our printer, Thomson-Shore, Inc., is a member of Green Press Initiative, a nonprofit program dedicated to supporting authors, publishers, and suppliers in their efforts to reduce their use of fiber obtained from endangered forests.

For more information, visit www.greenpressinitiative.org

Environmental impact estimates were made using the Environmental Defense Paper Calculator. For more information visit: www.papercalculator.org.